COCKPIT

AN ILLUSTRATED HISTORY OF
WORLD WAR II AIRCRAFT INTERIORS

BY
DONALD
NIJBOER

WITH PHOTOGRAPHS
BY DAN PATTERSON

INTRODUCTION BY
AIR VICE-MARSHAL
RON DICK, RAF (RET.)

The BOSTON
MILLS PRESS

A BOSTON MILLS PRESS BOOK

Copyright © 1998, 2006 Donald Nijboer
Photographs © Copyright 1998, 2006 Dan Patterson

Published by Boston Mills Press, 2006
132 Main Street, Erin, Ontario N0B 1T0
Tel: 519-833-2407 Fax: 519-833-2195
e-mail: books@bostonmillspress.com
www.bostonmillspress.com

In Canada:
Distributed by Firefly Books Ltd.
66 Leek Crescent
Richmond Hill, Ontario, Canada L4B 1H1

In the United States:
Distributed by Firefly Books (U.S.) Inc.
P.O. Box 1338, Ellicott Station
Buffalo, New York 14205

Library and Archives Canada Cataloguing in Publication

Nijboer, Donald, 1959–
Cockpit : an illustrated history of World War II aircraft interiors /
by Donald Nijboer ; with photographs by Dan Patterson ; introduction by Ron Dick.

Includes bibliographical references and index.
ISBN-13: 978-1-55046-488-7 (pbk.)
ISBN-10: 1-55046-488-4 (pbk.)

1. Airplanes — Cockpits.   2. Airplanes, Military — History.
I. Patterson, Dan, 1953– II. Title.

TL681.C6N54 1998   623.7'46049   C98-931099-X

Gift   623.7 PAT   # 5/27/09 OCLC

Publisher Cataloging-in-Publication Data (U.S.)

Nijboer, Donald, 1959–
Cockpit : an illustrated history of World War II aircraft interiors /
by Donald Nijboer ; with photographs by Dan Patterson ; introduction by Ron Dick.
Originally published: 1998.
[176] p. : col. photos. ; cm.
Includes bibliographical references and index.
Summary: The cockpits of World War II aircraft and the men who flew them.
ISBN-13: 978-1-55046-488-7 (pbk.)
ISBN-10: 1-55046-488-4 (pbk.)
1. Airplanes — Cockpits.   2. Airplanes, Military — History.
3. World War, 1939-1945 — Aerial operations. I. Patterson, Dan, 1953– . II. Title.
623.7/46049 dc22   TL681.C6N55 2006

The publisher gratefully acknowledges the financial support for our publishing program by
the Government of Canada through the Book Publishing Industry Development Program.

Design by The Unlimited Dream Company
Kevan (Magic) Buss, Creative Director
Printed in Hong Kong

If you would like to order copies of any of the cockpit photographs found in this book,
please contact Dan Patterson
6825 Peters Pike, Dayton, Ohio 45414
Tel 937-890-4639, Fax 937-890-7353

COCKPIT

COCKPIT

AN ILLUSTRATED HISTORY OF WORLD WAR II AIRCRAFT INTERIORS

This book is dedicated to
my father and mother,
Johan and Tonia Nijboer.

AUTHOR'S ACKNOWLEDGMENTS

This book would not have been possible without the help and support of my parents, Johan and Tonia Nijboer. I would like to thank John Denison and everyone at the Boston Mills Press and Stoddart Publishing. The hard work and talent of Kevan Buss turned a good book into a great one. A special thanks to Ron Dick, who not only provided the foreword and a "Pilot's Perspective" on the B-17, but whose name also opened many doors that would have remained closed to me if not for him. Thanks also to Stephen Grey for his time and for letting us crawl over his aircraft, to Jim Millan for his friendship and support, to Dan Patterson for his insights and connections, to Eric, Julia, and Andrea—yes, I *do* get a free book. To my sister, Marilyn, and brother, Gordon, thank you for your encouragement and inspiration.

The following people gave their time and expertise to help make this book possible. A grateful thanks to Lynda Spalding, Maureen Bracegirdle, Jonathan Peel, Suzanne Depoe, Kristine Kaske, Donna Pomes, Bill Rummer, Harvey Low, Garfield Ingram and Tennesse Katsuta of the International Plastic Modelers Society, Toronto Chapter; William Bartsch, Ed McKay, Larry Milberry, John Delaney, Doug Champlin, Ralph Royce, Dave Menard, David Ethell, Jeffrey L. Ethell, Stephen Payne, Ken Chilstrom, Robert Linnell, Fiona Hale, Robert C. Mikesh, John Weal, Tony Holmes, Philip Jarrett, Christine Gregory, Jennifer Barclay, Tom Atwood, Jeff Rushen and all the pilots who gave so freely of their time.

I would also like to thank the following museums, groups and individuals: the USAF Museum, the Imperial War Museum, the Fighter Collection, the Old Flying Machine Company, the Shuttleworth Collection, the Aerospace Museum, the Royal Air Force Museum, the National Aviation Museum, the Lone Star Flight Museum, the Champlin Fighter Aircraft Museum, the Aircraft Restoration Company, the National Air and Space Museum, Robert Spence and Butch Schroeder.

Grateful acknowledgment is made for permission to reprint excerpts from the following copyrighted books: *Those Who Fall*, by John Muirhead (1986), by permission of Random House Inc.; *The Straits of Messina*, by Johannes Steinhoff (1971), by permission of André Deutsch Limited.

PHOTOGRAPHER'S ACKNOWLEDGMENTS

Many thanks to Cheryl Terrill, my understanding friend; my kids, Nate, Brigitta, and Joe, who understand when Dad is out chasing airplanes again; my parents, Bill and Jane Patterson, who always told me that it was okay to follow my dreams; Ron Dick; and Kurt Weidner.

In the U.K., thanks to Clive Denney, David Henshie, Mark Hanna, Tim Fane, Steve Kingman, and Squadron Leader Paul Day.

In the U.S., thanks to Mike Vad bon Couer, Butch Schroeder, and Dave Tallichet.

Finally, thanks to the people at the USAF Museum: Maj. General Charles Metcalf, USAF (ret.) Director; Dave Menard; Bob Spaulding; Dick Tobias; Diana Bachert; Bob Bobbit; and Colonel Richard Uppstrom, Director (Ret.).

FOREWORD

In the world of aviation, the term *cockpit*, when applied to the crew compartments of military aircraft, or such high-performance private machines as warbirds, is particularly apt. It seems not nearly so appropriate for the flight deck of a Boeing 747 or the cabin of a Cessna 150. The aeronautical use of the word became common during the aerial confrontations of the First World War, and its original meaning remains unchanged. It defines the place where aviaton's fighting cocks face their challenges and fight their battles.

Cockpits reveal a great deal about their aircraft. The B-29's spacious greenhouse, for example, suits its strategic purpose. The simple layout and tight, neat confines of the Spitfire's cockpit are in perfect harmony with the fighter's small size and clean aerodynamics. Snuggled down among the Spitfire's modest instruments and controls, pilots felt almost fused with one of the world's great fighting aircraft, a machine refined until only the essentials for combat remained. The P-47's cockpit also matches its burly host, but in a different way. Roomy and bluntly functional, it corresponds with the aircraft's massive and rugged exterior. The weighty P-47 was very fast going downhill but was not as nimble as its smaller contemporaries. Its large cockpit and straight-line performance led some of its pilots to say that perhaps their most effective evasive action in combat would be to stand up and run around for a while.

For pilots, cockpits are almost womb-like in their capacity to offer comfort and reassurance. The act of strapping in tightly to the seat helps to integrate pilot and machine, the one becoming the soul of the other in the process. This transformation having taken place, the pilot's hands find encouragement from the way they fall naturally to stick and throttle. They move and the machine responds, offering full three-dimensional freedom. It is no wonder that cockpits hold an irresistible fascination for those who have experienced their magic. They offer an escape from terrestrial bondage and a level of exhilaration that is hard to match. As if that were not enough, they also provide the ultimate ego boost, and we all need that from time to time.

— AIR VICE-MARSHAL RON DICK,
CB, FRAeS, RAF (Ret.)

PHOTOGRAPHER'S PREFACE

Donald Nijboer and I share a fascination with the aircraft that made history during the Second World War. I spent countless hours as a kid reading about the great air battles of the Second World War and the aircrews that flew and fought in them. I built models of my favourite airplanes, trying to imagine myself inside the cockpit of the B-17 or the Spitfire. Plastic aerial armadas occupied the ceiling of my bedroom, suspended by a network of interlaced fishing line. I learned a lesson about knot tying when one of my novice attempts gave way and an entire air division came crashing to the floor. In spite of such setbacks I never lost that fascination.

In taking the photographs for this book I have tried to satisfy my curiosity about the pilot's environment. I asked myself the same questions with each airplane. Where does the pilot sit? How tough is it to see ahead, to the side, and perhaps most important, to the rear? Where are the flight controls, the throttle, the flight instruments, the fuel gauges? How noisy would it have been? In the case of the Messerschmitt Bf 109, how did the pilot actually get into the cockpit and close the hood. For each airplane came different answers. The evolution of the war changed how airplanes were designed and built, and the pilots had to adapt to each progression—bigger engines, more and higher calibre armaments, increasingly complex systems—while trying to stay alive to fight another day.

If you happen to come along when I am working on one of these books, and you happen to see this 44-year-old guy sitting in the pilot's seat, looking around inside the cockpit and through the canopy, you're really seeing a 14-year-old who has realized that dreams come true.

— Dan Patterson

10

INTRODUCTION

At the outbreak of the Second World War, the biplane was obsolete and the idea of fighting in an open cockpit was a thing of the past. New innovations in aircraft construction and aircraft systems produced the enclosed cockpit. Flying these new aircraft was far more demanding and required a greater degree of training. The cluttered, claustrophobic cockpit was rarely designed for comfort, and more powerful engines, variable-pitch propellers, variable flaps, and retractable landing gear added to the number of controls. Riding behind an ear-shattering 2,000-horsepower engine proved to be an exhilarating and sometimes deadly experience. Developed before supersonic designs and computers, the cockpits in this book depict the last generation of aircraft in which the pilot could feel totally in control.

Cockpit reveals what very few of us ever get to see. It is also a tribute to the people who restore and preserve these wonderful aircraft. Without their dedication and hard work this book would not have been possible.

At the heart of this book is the wonderful photography of Dan Patterson. Dan's technique, attention to detail, and enthusiasm for the subject matter is self-evident. Dan's photograph of a B-17 cockpit, which I saw for the first time at the USAF Museum, proved to be the inspiration for this book. Working with Dan has been a great pleasure.

Additionally, both veteran pilots and pilots who fly some of these aircraft today have contributed to this book. Their wartime recollections and rich insights paint a vivid picture of what it was like to fly and fight in these cockpits.

Not all of the cockpits represented in this book are stock. Some are in various stages of restoration, while others are flying examples. In some cases instruments have been added, while others have been moved for safety and convenience. It was not always possible to track down and photograph the most ideal cockpit.

Be that as it may, what we *have* managed to accomplish is something quite striking. Rare cockpits, including the Me 410, the Kawanishi Shiden, the Kawasaki Ki-100, the Ju 87, the Seversky P-35, and the Hawker Typhoon, are illustrated here for the first time in one volume. This is your chance to sit in the cockpit. Enjoy.

— DONALD NIJBOER

Far ahead of us, the sky looked different. There was a band of brown haze from eighteen thousand feet up to about twenty-three thousand. It was not easy to see; you had to know what you were looking for; I knew what it was; I had seen it before. Flak. The dirty strings from a flak barrage drifted in the cold wind. Less than five minutes ago a group had gone through it, and now the shreds of smoke were fading and were barely visible. A black column was rising from the ground in the southeast. Someone had hit something big, something that had violently blown...We were beginning our run.

"There was not a daub of black in the sky; for a blessed moment we made our slow, inexorable passage across it unchallenged. Seconds passed. When it came, it came like a mighty shout, a malediction hurling up at us through four miles of twisting wind. They were everywhere; the dark flowers of flak were everywhere. Four successive shells exploded in front of my right wing, and I felt the wheel tremble in my hands. An orange core glared out of a shroud of smoke in front of me. Our plane shuddered against the concussion of two bursts underneath us.... My left wing dropped away from me, and I drove my foot hard against the right rudder to bring it up. I didn't pray. I didn't curse. I didn't think. I crouched in my cave of instruments, tubes and wires. **"**

— JOHN MUIRHEAD,
THOSE WHO FALL

GLOSTER GLADIATOR   FAIREY SWORDFISH   HAWKER SEA HURRICANE   SUPERMARINE SPITFIRE

UNITED KINGDOM

BRISTOL BLENHEIM

BRISTOL BEAUFIGHTER

DE HAVILLAND MOSQUITO

HAWKER TYPHOON

AVRO LANCASTER

G L O S T E R

GLADIATOR

THE GLOSTER GLADIATOR WAS THE LAST
BIPLANE FIGHTER TO ENTER FRONTLINE RAF SERVICE
AND ONE OF THE FIRST TO SEE ACTION.

Through the early 1930s, bomber designs remained the same. These slow, fabric-covered biplanes were lightly armed and carried a small bomb load. At the time, the biplane fighters that were being built or under development were considered more than adequate to defeat these lumbering giants. Then, in a few short years, everything changed. New, sleek monoplanes with retractable undercarriages and enclosed cockpits appeared. Able to fly higher and faster, these new machines spelled the end of the biplane fighter.

Fighter procurement is an exercise in predicting the future. One has to look towards a future rather than a present threat. In July 1935, less than a year after the first prototype had flown, 23 Gladiator Is were ordered by the RAF. Obsolete before it took to the air, the Gladiator was an excellent biplane fighter, with an enclosed cockpit. Its performance was credible, and, when operated in areas free of enemy fighters, it gave a good account of itself in the early months of the Second World War.

In September 1938, frontline RAF Fighter Command strength consisted of 573 obsolete biplanes and a mere 93 Hurricanes and Spitfires. By 1939, most Gladiator squadrons were re-equipped with Hurricanes, Defiants, and Spitfires. The few Gladiators that remained in frontline service would be the first RAF fighters used to take the fight to the enemy.

On April 9, 1940, Norway was invaded. The carefully executed German plan landed troops in half a dozen coastal cities. Soon after, the French and British sent a small, ill-equipped force to reinforce the Norwegian Army. That force included 18 Gloster Gladiators from 263 Squadron. A hastily prepared strip was located near Aandalsnes, in central Norway. Taking off from the aircraft carrier HMS *Glorious*,

the 18 Gladiators landed on April 24. By the end of the day, 10 of the 18 aircraft were out of operation. On May 21, 263 Squadron, with replacement Gladiators, moved to a new airstrip at Narvik. There they fought alongside Hurricanes from 46 Squadron, but by the beginning of June the end was in sight. On June 3, evacuations of Narvik began, and the surviving Gladiators of 263 Squadron were flown back to HMS *Glorious*.

During the Battle of France, the British committed the Advanced Air Striking Force. This force consisted of Fairey Battle light bombers, Blenheims, Lysanders, Hurricanes, and two squadrons of Gladiators. In concert with the Hurricane and French fighter squadrons, the damage inflicted on the Luftwaffe was enormous, but the numerical superiority of the Luftwaffe became overwhelming and the Gladiator bases were overrun.

Soon after the Battle of France, the Battle of Britain began. The only remaining home-based Gladiator squadrons were 247 Squadron, at Exeter, and 804 Fleet Air Arm Squadron, at Wick.

In the Mediterranean, Malta's strategic importance grew as military operations in and around the island began to take shape. In 1940, the island's fighter defence consisted of three Fleet Air Arm Sea Gladiators. Their efforts were so effective that the Regia Aeronautica (Italian Air Force) overestimated Malta's fighter strength, concluding that there were 25 in operation!

The Gloster Gladiator saw service in Europe, Malta, Greece, Crete, and the Western Desert. Although clearly outclassed by modern monoplane fighters, the Gladiator always managed to give a good account of itself. After being withdrawn from operational service, the Gladiator was used for meteorological reconnaissance flights.

RIGHT: MET. FLIGHT GLADIATOR TAKING OFF. *INSET*: SQUADRON LEADER PATRICK HUNTER DUNN IN THE COCKPIT OF HIS GLADIATOR. *ABOVE*: A GLADIATOR OF THE RAF PATROLLING THE SKIES ABOVE BARDIA DURING THE LAST PHASE OF THE BATTLE.

THE PILOT'S
P E R S P E C T I V E
ROGER BAILEY
THE SHUTTLEWORTH COLLECTION

The cockpit of the Gladiator offers good size and easy access, with let-down panels on each side. Because of the fumes in the cockpit, closing the canopy was not very popular, except when it was very cold. Of course, in squadron service, pilots would have breathed oxygen all the time.

In terms of size it's pretty good for a British airplane. But, typical for a British fighter, there is no real floor, so if you drop a map it will disappear.

Going around the cockpit, from left to right, there's a large elevator trim wheel. The gearing is good and it's easy to move. Up from there you have the throttle box, throttle and mixture control, and carburetor heater control. The throttle is nice, but the boost gauge is on the far side of the cockpit. It's pretty easy to overboost the engine if you're not watching carefully. The ignition switches and the cylinder head temperature are on the left-hand side of the cockpit, next to the oxygen regulator and the gunsight selector. All the rest of engine instruments, or most of them, are over to the right. It would have made an awful lot of sense to have them all in one place.

The centre panel is pretty much the standard blind flying panel, but not quite. The view through the canopy is okay, but unless you know this airplane has an adjustable seat, it can get you into trouble. On my first flight I was amazed at how little I could see. Nobody told me it had an adjustable seat! The cockpit is typical of the period; there's not a lot of logic to it. There's plenty of room and I can actually get full aileron between my knees. That's very unusual in a British airplane.

GLOSTER GLADIATOR Mk I
SHUTTLEWORTH COLLECTION, ENGLAND

1. CONTROL COLUMN
2. GUN BUTTON
3. MIXTURE & THROTTLE CONTROL
4. FUEL CONTENTS GAUGE
5. CARBURETTOR CUTOUT
6. FUEL COCK
7. OXYGEN GAUGE
8. AIRSPEED INDICATOR
9. LIGHTING RHEOSTAT
10. ARTIFICIAL HORIZON
11. RATE OF CLIMB INDICATOR
12. ALTIMETER
13. DIRECTION INDICATOR
14. TURN AND BANK INDICATOR
15. RPM GAUGE
16. BOOST PRESSURE GAUGE
17. OIL TEMP GAUGE
18. OIL COOLER CONTROL
19. PRIMER
20. STARTER BUTTON
21. OIL PRESSURE GAUGE
22. FUEL PRESSURE GAUGE
23. COMPASS
24. RUDDER PEDALS
25. PILOT HEAT SWITCH
26. STARTING MAGNETO SWITCH

WITH A CHART SPREAD ON THE WING OF A GLADIATOR, THE COMMANDING OFFICER GIVES PILOTS THEIR INSTRUCTIONS BEFORE TAKE-OFF.

FAIREY
SWORDFISH

ALTHOUGH HOPELESSLY OBSOLETE WHEN THE SECOND WORLD WAR STARTED, MORE SWORDFISH WERE OPERATIONAL ON THE LAST DAY OF THE WAR THAN ON THE FIRST!

When accepted into service with the Fleet Air Arm in 1936, the Swordfish was an anachronism. Newer types, such as the sleek monoplane Spitfire and the sturdy Hurricane, were appearing with enclosed cockpits and retractable undercarriages. In contrast, the Swordfish, a direct descendant of the Sopwith Camel, SE-5 Scout and all other First World War aircraft, was a fabric-covered biplane with a fixed undercarriage, struts and wires, and an open cockpit. It was quickly nicknamed "String Bag" by its crews.

First flown in 1933, the Swordfish had a maximum speed of 139 miles per hour (224 km/h), with a torpedo. The two-man crew consisted of a pilot and the observer/gunner. Armament consisted of one fixed forward-firing Vickers light machine gun and one rear-mounted flexible Lewis light machine gun. Incredibly easy to fly, and with a landing speed of just 67 miles per hour (108 km/h), the Swordfish could operate from the smallest carriers under the most appalling conditions.

Swordfish from the HMS *Illustrious* would lead the first major carrier strike of the War — and history. On November 11, 1940, 170 miles from Taranto Harbour, in Italy, 22 Swordfish lifted off the carrier deck. After more than two hours in the air, the first wave of 12 aircraft attacked. In the harbour were 6 battleships, 9 cruisers and more than 25 destroyers, 16 submarines and a score of small vessels. Suddenly, parachute flares transformed night into day and the over 300 fixed anti-aircraft guns came to life. The Battle of Taranto was not a surprise attack, and the success of the Swordfish says much about the superb flying skill of its pilots. Through intense flak, the attacking Swordfish managed to sink the new battleship *Conte de Cavour* and wreck

two others. With just two losses, half of the Italian fleet was put out of commission for four months.

In May 1941, the Swordfish would meet another capital ship, this time the powerful *Bismarck*. As darkness approached on May 26, 15 Swordfish took off from the *Ark Royal*. Hours later, the *Bismarck* was sighted and the attacked commenced. The attack was not coordinated, and through heavy flak, the aircraft closed in to point-blank range and launched their torpedoes. The *Bismarck* was hit twice. One torpedo struck the massive armoured belt; the other exploded near the ship's propellers and jammed the rudders. Unable to manoeuvre, the *Bismarck* was soon destroyed by the pursuing British battleships and cruisers.

In 1944, the Swordfish was still operational and in greater numbers than when the war first started. In the Atlantic, the Swordfish served in a dozen squadrons, aboard the escort carriers *Activity, Archer, Avenger, Battler, Biter, Campania, Chaser, Dasher, Hunter, Rapana, Stalker, Striker, Tracker,* and *Vindex.* The operational conditions were appalling, particulary while escorting convoys to the Soviet Union.

Obsolete by any standard, the Swordfish managed to become one of the most successful torpedo bombers of the Second World War—success that was due to its sturdiness, simplicity, and superb deck-landing qualities. During the War, the Swordfish would establish two amazing records: most operational hours flown, and greatest tonnage of enemy shipping destroyed. When war broke out, there were 140 Swordfish on strength with the Fleet Air Arm. In 1944, its last year of production, 420 were produced. The last operational squadron was 836 Squadron, which was disbanded on May 21, 1945.

RIGHT: MK II SWORDFISH LIFTS OFF FROM HMS *TRACKER.* INSET: CLOSE-UP OF SWORDFISH MK I, IN FLIGHT.
ABOVE: SWORDFISH PREPARES FOR TAKE-OFF.

THE PILOT'S
P E R S P E C T I V E
LIEUTENANT
PHILIP FOULDS
DSC RCNVR (RET.)

When I first flew the Swordfish, I was surprised at how big it was. The wing span is 45 feet (14 m) and the upper mainplane sits over 12 feet (3.6 m) from the deck. The open cockpit was very spacious for the pilot but less so for the observer and gunner in back. Of course, the all-round view was exceptional, but it was a very drafty cockpit. In fact, the gunner and observer could actually stand when they needed to, but most of the time they were hunched down to protect themselves from the wind.

The flight instruments were of a conventional layout, and straightforward. The cockpit was so big that you had no difficulty identifying individual flight instruments or controls. One thing the Swordfish didn't have was a radio altimeter. To drop a torpedo correctly you should be flying at 50 feet (15 m) above the water, which was a judgement call even after early, unreliable, radio altimeters came along. The Swordfish was a very simple aircraft to fly. Its fixed undercarriage, fixed pitch prop, and no flaps made you feel like you were riding a motorbike. It was very stable in the air, with wonderful stall characteristics.

After torpedo school I was sent out to South Africa to a Pool Squadron for the Eastern Fleet. There we flew rehearsals and the occasional anti-submarine patrol, all in summer weather.

Flying in the open cockpit was a different matter for crews in the North Atlantic. Sometimes chilled crews had to be lifted out of the cockpit after a three- or four-hour anti-submarine patrol.

In one of the last Swordfish operations of the war, they were used to attack some ships in a Norwegian fjord. While the Swordfish flew into the fjord, our Avenger squadron flew anti-submarine patrols. Some might think it should have been the other way around, but the Swordfish's manoeuvrability was well suited to the tight confines of the fjord.

The Swordfish was a remarkable aircraft to fly. It was a real winner.

FAIREY SWORDFISH Mk II
ROBERT SPENCE, MUIRKIRK, ONTARIO

1. LIGHTING SWITCH-PANEL
2. MIXTURE CONTROL LEVER
3. THROTTLE LEVER
4. INERTIA STARTER CLUTCH CONTROL RING
5. AUTOMATIC BOOST CONTROL CUT-OUT
6. BOOST PRESSURE GAUGE
7. AIR PRESSURE GAUGE
8. LANDING LAMP DEFLECTION CONTROL
9. BOMB JETTISON SWITCH
10. ASI
11. COMPASS LAMPS DIMMER SWITCH
12. COMPASS LAMPS TWO-PIN SOCKET
13. COMPASS
14. TORPEDO SIGHT CONTROL SWITCH
15. STARTER SWITCH
16. DIRECTION INDICATOR
17. ARTIFICIAL HORIZON
18. ENGINE SPEED INDICATOR
19. PRIMING PUMP
20. ALTIMETER
21. TURN AND BANK INDICATOR
22. FUEL PRESSURE WARNING LIGHT
23. OIL PRESSURE GAUGE
24. OIL TEMP GAUGE
25. CONTROL COLUMN
26. GUN BUTTON
27. OIL BY-PASS VALVE CONTROL
28. AIR INTAKE SHUTTER CONTROL

PILOT OF "DIRTY DICK I" PREPARES FOR TAKE-OFF.

HAWKER
HURRICANE

RUGGED AND VERSATILE, THE HAWKER HURRICANE
WAS A REMARKABLE FIGHTER THAT SAW SERVICE
ON EVERY FRONT ON WHICH THE RAF WAS ENGAGED.

The Hawker Hurricane was the RAF's first modern monoplane fighter. During the Battle of Britain, it destroyed more aircraft than the famous Spitfire did. Compared to the Spitfire, the Hurricane could be re-armed and refuelled in half the time. This was a vital factor in the fighter's success and contributed greatly to the Hurricane's impressive score.

First flown in September 1935, the Hurricane exceeded 300 miles per hour (483 km/h) in level flight and was heavily armed, with eight machine guns. In many ways the Hurricane was a "transitional" airplane, bridging the gap from fabric and wood to the new aluminium monocoque construction. The fuselage was made of wood and fabric, strengthened by a metal tube framework; the wings were made of aluminum. This mixed construction allowed the Hurricane to sustain heavy damage. Exploding cannon shells could cause horrific damage to metal-skinned aircraft, but the Hurricane could be easily repaired and returned to operational service quickly.

By September 1939, 18 squadrons were fully equipped, twice as many as there were Spitfire squadrons. In the first eight months of the war, Hurricane squadrons bore the brunt of the fighting.

ABOVE: AN ALL-BLACK NIGHT-FIGHTER HURRICANE MK IIC.
BELOW: HURRICANE MK IIDS PREPARING FOR TAKE-OFF, NORTH AFRICA 1943. *RIGHT*: A YOUNG HURRICANE PILOT READY FOR TAKE-OFF.

After the fall of France, the Hurricane was credited with 80 percent of the RAF victories, and at the beginning of the Battle of Britain, 29 squadrons of Hurricanes were ready.

Although completely outclassed by the Bf 109, the Hurricane continued to soldier on. The Hurricane was adapted for many roles, including night-fighter, tank buster, reconnaissance, and ground attack; it would also provide the Fleet Air Arm with its first carrier fighter, turning in a performance comparable to that of land-based Axis planes. At the end of 1941, the Fleet Air Arm accepted a number of ex-Battle of Britain Hurricanes. These old aircraft were strengthened and reinforced for carrier operations and pressed into service. In August 1942, Sea Hurricanes provided effective fighter cover over the vital Malta convoys and provided support during the Allied landings in Madagascar. In the Atlantic, Sea Hurricanes flown from MAC and CAM ships were able to prevent numerous attacks by marauding Focke-Wulf 200 long-range Condors.

As the air war evolved and ground attack became an integral part of the land battle, the Hawker Hurricane gained a new lease on life. Armed with bombs, rockets, and 40-mm cannons, the Hurricane became a formidable ground-attack aircraft. In North Africa, the Hurricane was the only Western aircraft to be armed with heavy cannons. As a result, it was pressed into the flying tank-buster role. In the "forgotten war," in Burma, it was the Hurricane that played a leading role. In June 1943, 23 squadrons were equipped and ready for the land offensive against the Japanese. In the following year, the Indian Air Force contributed another 14 squadrons. Its rugged construction, legendary stability and excellent versatility made it ideal for the primitive jungle conditions.

The Hawker Hurricane was one of the few single-seat fighters to see service in almost every part of the world, including Abyssinia, Egypt, Libya, Greece, Crete, Malta, Aden, Tunisia, Palestine, Syria, Russia, Italy, Sicily, Iceland, the North Atlantic, India, Burma, Java, and Sumatra. After six years of global war, the Hawker Hurricane was still in operational service with three RAF and eight Indian Air Force squadrons.

THE PILOT'S
P E R S P E C T I V E
DAVID MACKAY
THE SHUTTLEWORTH COLLECTION

My initial impression of the Hurricane cockpit is that it is disorganized. Wherever you look, you see controls. At first, it looks as if it was just sort of thrown together. You'd have to be careful not to drop anything, because you wouldn't get it back. Once you become more familiar with the cockpit, everything falls pretty much into place. Compared to the P-51, it looks like a previous generation of aircraft, more like something from the 1930s, which, of course, is when it was first flown.

The first thing that catches your eye when you sit down is the stick, which sits very high, so that your hand is in line with the top of your chest. The blind flying panel is pretty much conventional. It's well laid out in that you've got your horizon in the middle and your speed to the left. Your altimeter is down below the airspeed indicator, but you've got your vertical speed indicator to the right-hand side and your magnetic compass down below. Over on the right side you've got the engine instruments—boost, oil pressure, oil temperature, radiator temperature— and you've also got the fuel gauges, fuel pressure, and fuel tanks.

The cockpit is quite roomy up to about hand level, but it's quite narrow near the sills. The field of view is very good. The difference between the Hurricane and the Spitfire is that the Hurricane's nose is well curved and not quite as long. It's curved downward at the front and side, so your peripheral view when looking forward is much better than in a Spitfire and better than a lot of other Second World War aircraft. From a cockpit point of view, it's fine. From a performance point of view, I'd rather fight in a Spitfire.

SEA HURRICANE Mk Ib
SHUTTLEWORTH COLLECTION, ENGLAND

1. AIRSPEED INDICATOR
2. ARTIFICIAL HORIZON
3. RATE OF CLIMB/ DESCENT INDICATOR
4. ALTIMETER
5. DIRECTION INDICATOR
6. TURN AND BANK INDICATOR
7. GUN BUTTON
8. CONTROL COLUMN
9. UNDERCARRIAGE INDICATOR
10. ENGINE SPEED INDICATOR
11. BOOST GAUGE
12. FUEL CONTENTS GAUGE SELECTOR SWITCH
13. OIL PRESSURE GAUGES
14. FUEL CONTENTS GAUGE
15. RADIATOR TEMP GAUGE
16. OIL TEMP GAUGE
17. MAGNETIC COMPASS
18. UNDERCARRIAGE SAFETY SELECTOR CATCH
19. UNDERCARRIAGE AND FLAP SELECTOR SWITCH
20. GUNSIGHT
21. OXYGEN SUPPLY GAUGE
22. OXYGEN SUPPLY FLOW METER
23. SIGNALLING SWITCHBOX
24. GUN CAMERA SWITCH
25. CYLINDER PRIMING PUMP
26. BEAM APPROACH MASTER SWTICH

SEA HURRICANES ON HMS *VICTORIOUS*, JUNE 1942.

SUPERMARINE
SPITFIRE

"In weaponry terms, the Hurricane was a broadsword,
the Bf 109 a spear, while the Spitfire was a rapier,
an instrument of delicacy and precision."
— Mike Spick, *Supermarine Spitfire*

When Supermarine prototype K5054 first took flight, its promise as a fighter was evident in its sleek, elegant lines. The frontal area of the famous Merlin engine and the size of the pilot were the determining factors in creating one of the smallest cockpits of the war. Its narrow confines fit a burly pilot like a glove. On early models, the canopy was a one-piece straight Perspex sliding type. For taller pilots this was a problem, but early in production the canopy was bulged, providing pilots with extra headroom. This modification proved a huge advantage when compared to the Bf 109's cockpit. In complete contrast, the 109's hood hinged sideways, could not accommodate a tall pilot, and the heavy metal framework created blind spots, hindering the pilot's view.

The Spitfire I was the first version to enter service, and in 1938, 1,583 were built. The first squadron to receive the new fighter, designated Mk IA, was 19 Squadron, RAF Duxford. This model equipped most squadrons during the Battle of Britain. For the next six years, Spitfires (and Seafires) flew on every operational front. Its versatility was legendary. In combat, the Spitfire was equal to or better than the Bf 109. Its greatest advantage was its faster rate of roll and tighter turning radius. In 1941, Spitfires took on the Luftwaffe over Europe; Sholto Douglas, the new Commander in Chief of RAF Fighter Command, called it "leaning forward into France." In operations known as "Circuses," up to 22 squadrons of Spitfires escorted a handful of bombers into Northern France. These operations proved disappointing, and when the German Focke Wulf Fw 190 entered service, the Spitfire V was totally outclassed. As losses mounted, the Spitfire IX was rushed into service. Fitted with the Merlin 60 series engine, the Mk IX matched the Fw 190 in performance and soon redressed the balance.

In the Pacific, the Mitsubishi A6M Zero proved to be the Spitfire's equal. Japanese advances in 1943 brought their bombers and fighters to within striking distance of Darwin, Australia. A wing of Spitfire VCs was sent to oppose them. The Spitfire pilots were in for a rude shock. In early 1943, a large Japanese raid was intercepted over the Timor Sea. The ensuing battle resulted in the loss of five Spitfires for five Zeros and a bomber. When the Spitfire pilots tried to turn with the Zeros, they quickly found themselves on the receiving end. Turning with a Zero at moderate to low speeds proved fatal. Dive and zoom tactics were soon adopted to counter future Japanese raids.

The year 1943 saw the introduction of the first Griffon-engine Spitfire. The F.XII served in only two squadrons and was quickly followed by the Spitfire XIV, which was markedly superior to the Fw 190A at all operational heights. It was faster, with a superior rate of climb and was slightly better in a dive. Not until the introduction of the Fw 190D "long nose" did the Luftwaffe possess a fighter roughly equal to the XIV.

D-Day saw the Spitfire flying in many different roles: bomber escort, fighter sweep, fighter-bomber, naval gunfire spotting, reconnaissance, and air-sea rescue. Allied fighters flew more than 200,000 sorties between June 6, 1944, and September 5, 1944, many of which were flown by Spitfires.

At the end of the war, Spitfires were still being produced. The final variant was the Mk 24. When compared to the early Mk I, the Mk 24 was 25 percent faster, climbed nearly twice as fast, and had a service ceiling of 43,000 feet (13,115 m). But by this time, jetfighter technology made the piston-engine fighter obsolete.

Left: Spitfire Vs of 417 Squadron Royal Canadian Air Force flying in loose formation over Tunisia.
Above: Spitfire Mk IX over Italy.

THE PILOT'S
PERSPECTIVE
DAVE BOYD
SQUADRON LEADER RCAF

I went overseas in October 1941. In November, I was posted to OTU, where I flew Spitfire Is and IIs until February. Later that month, I was posted to 412 Squadron and flew the improved Mk V.

When I first sat in a Spitfire cockpit it seemed rather rudimentary compared to the Harvard. The RAF didn't pay as much attention to switches and instrumentation as the Americans did. Compared to the Harvard cockpit, the Spitfire was very small, but you got used to it. For an average-size person it was quite comfortable.

The blind flying panel was standard in all RAF aircraft, and I found the instrumentation to be well laid out. The throttle control and friction were excellent and the trim control was very good. The only significant cockpit problem in the Spitfire was the landing gear control, which was located on the right side, with the throttle on the left. Having to change hands on take-off was a little tough, particularly when you were taking off in formation. On the early Spits, the undercarriage was raised and lowered by a hydraulic hand pump on the right-hand side; for the inexperienced pilot this resulted in a "porpoising" flight after take-off.

The early canopies were flat sided, which made it tough to see what was behind you. That was improved greatly in 1942 with the introduction of the bulged hood. To keep the canopy polished and to remove scratches, we used to use jeweller's rouge, a fine grinding compound for polishing metal and brass.

The Spitfire cockpit was simple, comfortable, and snug. It was normally unheated, and our heavy Irving jackets proved to be too bulky. You couldn't turn to see what was behind you. Generally, we wore a battle dress, with a sweater underneath in cold weather.

I found the Spitfire to be a beautiful airplane to fly, especially the Mk IXe (LF), which was generally superior to the latest Bf 109s and Fw 190s.

SUPERMARINE SPITFIRE Mk II
BATTLE OF BRITAIN MEMORIAL FLIGHT

1. AIRSPEED INDICATOR
2. ARTIFICIAL HORIZON
3. RATE OF CLIMB INDICATOR
4. ALTIMETER
5. DIRECTION INDICATOR
6. TURNING INDICATOR
7. VENTILATOR CONTROL
8. OIL PRESSURE GAUGE
9. BOOST PRESSURE GAUGE
10. OIL TEMP GAUGE
11. RADIATOR TEMP GAUGE
12. FUEL CONTENTS GAUGE
13. PRIMING PUMP
14. FUEL COCK
15. MAGNETIC COMPASS
16. GUN BUTTON
17. CONTROL COLUMN
18. ENGINE STARTING BUTTON
19. COCKPIT LAMP DIMMER SWITCHES
20. RADIATOR FLAP CONTROL LEVER
21. FLAP CONTROL
22. INDICATOR LIGHT
23. VENTILATOR GAUGE
24. AMMETER
25. ENGINE SPEED INDICATOR

WARMING UP
A SPITFIRE MK V.

B R I S T O L
BLENHEIM

In the early years of the war, the Blenheim's greatest virtues were its availability and its reliability. Unfortunately, throughout its operational career it could be described neither as effective nor as decisive.

In the years leading up to the Second World War, the RAF began a process of modernization. A whole new range of modern aircraft was introduced into service. One of those aircraft was the Bristol Blenheim. The Blenheim was a fast twin-engine monoplane bomber, with a speed greater than biplane fighters in service at the time. It reached a top speed of 240 miles per hour (386 km/h), which proved to be some 40 miles per hour (64 km/h) better than that of the fastest fighter to date. The first two prototypes, which were actually production aircraft, flew on June 25, 1937. Fitted with variable-pitch propellers, the Blenheim would reach an impressive 307 miles per hour (494 km/h)!

When war broke out, the Bristol Blenheim was employed in many roles never envisioned by its designer. With the war situation changing rapidly, the Blenheim was used as a bomber, a long-range fighter, a night-fighter, and a reconnaissance aircraft. At the beginning of the hostilities, the RAF had 32 Blenheim squadrons on strength. On September 3, 1939, a Blenheim flew the first RAF mission of the war. Aircraft from 139 Squadron flew a reconnaissance mission over the German naval base at Wilhelmshaven. Shortly after, a bombing mission was mounted; Blenheims from 107 and 110 Squadrons bombed the naval vessels in the harbour. With no vessels seriously damaged and five aircraft lost, the results were not encouraging.

On November 28, 1939, the first fighter versions of the Blenheim saw action. Armed with a belly pack of four 0.303-inch machine guns, the Blenheims from 25 and 601 Squadrons strafed the seaplane base at Borkum, off the northwest coast of Germany.

On April 8, 1940, Germany invaded Denmark and Norway. Blenheim long-range fighters from 254 Squadron were very active throughout the campaign. A variety of missions was flown, including long-range patrolling to protect shipping, strafing of German-occupied airfields, and attacks on German bombers and maritime patrol aircraft. The results were unimpressive, with 254 Squadron losing approximately the same number of aircraft as they destroyed.

When the German Blitzkrieg stormed over France and the low countries in May 1940, Allied bomber losses that included Blenheims were appalling. Unable to stem the German tide, many Blenheim squadrons were destroyed or returned to England with great loss.

In July 1940, the Blenheim was the first aircraft to be fitted with the new AI Mk III Airborne Interception Radar. Success was soon to follow. On July 22, the first night-fighter kill was scored. But the Blenheim's night-fighter role was short-lived. With the added equipment, its speed was slow, leaving it only marginally faster than the German bombers it was sent out to chase. It was soon replaced by the superior Bristol Beaufighter.

In the Far East, the Blenheim suffered more losses. On December 8, the Japanese attacked Malaya and once again the Blenheim was thrust into battle. By the end of the first day of operations, most of the Blenheims had been destroyed on the ground.

The Blenheim had a poor operational record. As a bomber, its performance was mediocre; it was unable to defend itself and, as a result, it was unpopular with its crews. Nevertheless, the Blenheim did see service in some of the most inhospitable theatres of war and continued bombing operations in the Far East until 1943.

Above: A Blenheim Mk I in flight above the clouds. *Right*: Blenheims of 139 Squadron flying over France, 1940. *Inset*: A Blenheim Mk IV warms up its engines prior to take-off.

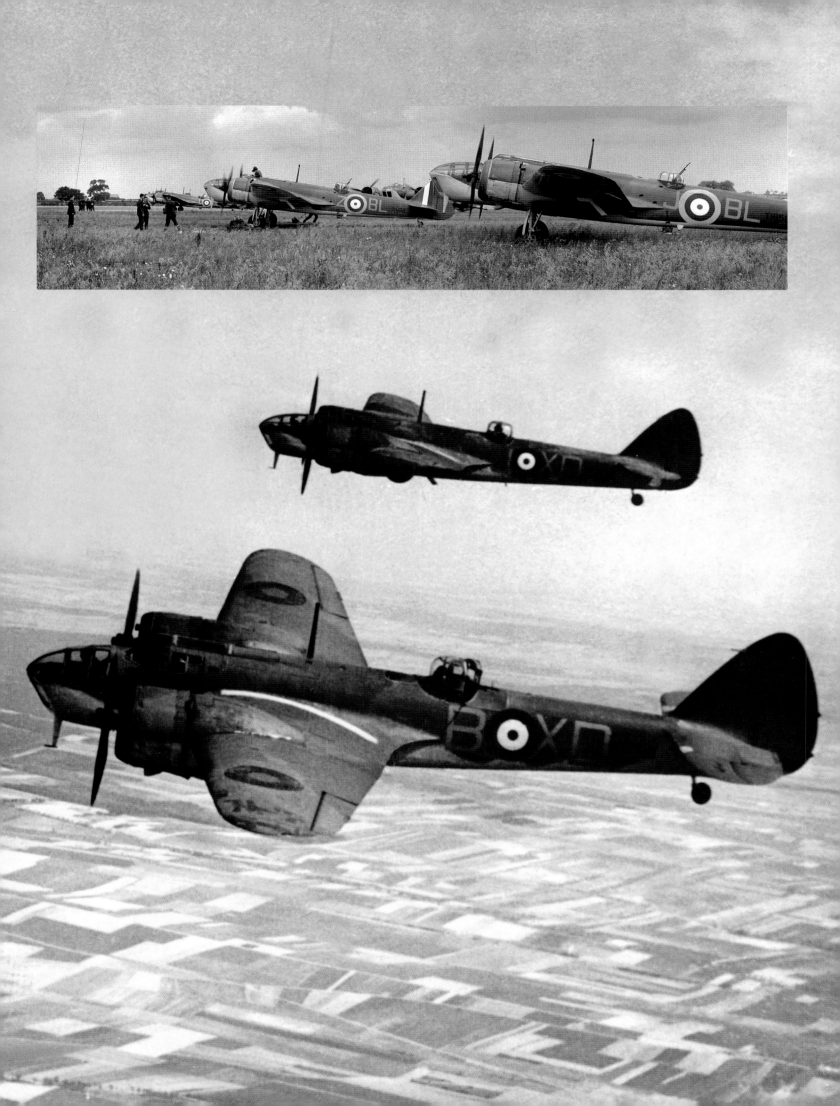

THE PILOT'S
P E R S P E C T I V E
RAYNE SCHULTZ
GROUP CAPTAIN
RCAF (RET.), DFC, OMM, CD

In the Blenheim, there was lots of room in the seat. The switches were typically British, and not too well organized as far as I can remember. On one of the Marks, I think it was the Mk I, we only had two-speed propellers, not constant-speed. The Bisely, and most of the Mk IVs, had constant speed props. To change from fine to coarse, you had to reach around behind you and pull these knobs. It was the most awkward thing you could imagine. That was one of the last things you did on pre-check before take-off. First, you had to make sure your gills were in trail, not wide open, because of the drag. The flaps were set properly and the pitch was set to fine for take-off. In an emergency, reaching around for the pitch control was especially difficult, and I think these were non-feathering props.

The instrumentation in the Blenheim was very good. The British had made a firm decision a long time before to go to the standard blind flying panel. That carried right through to the seventies. It made particular sense if you were going into the night fighting or night flying.

The Blenheim cockpit was roomy, like a house with lots of windows. As for comfort and temperature, it was dreadful. The layout of the various switches and controls, especially the landing gear, was also terrible. In order to get in and out of the aircraft, you had to stand on the frame cover of the landing gear control. It was usually all bent and cracked, and when you reached down and lifted the thing up you could cut your hand. I think everyone cut their hands sooner or later.

To sum up, the Blenheim cockpit had an awful lot of sharp corners. It was drafty and cold, but it was all right.

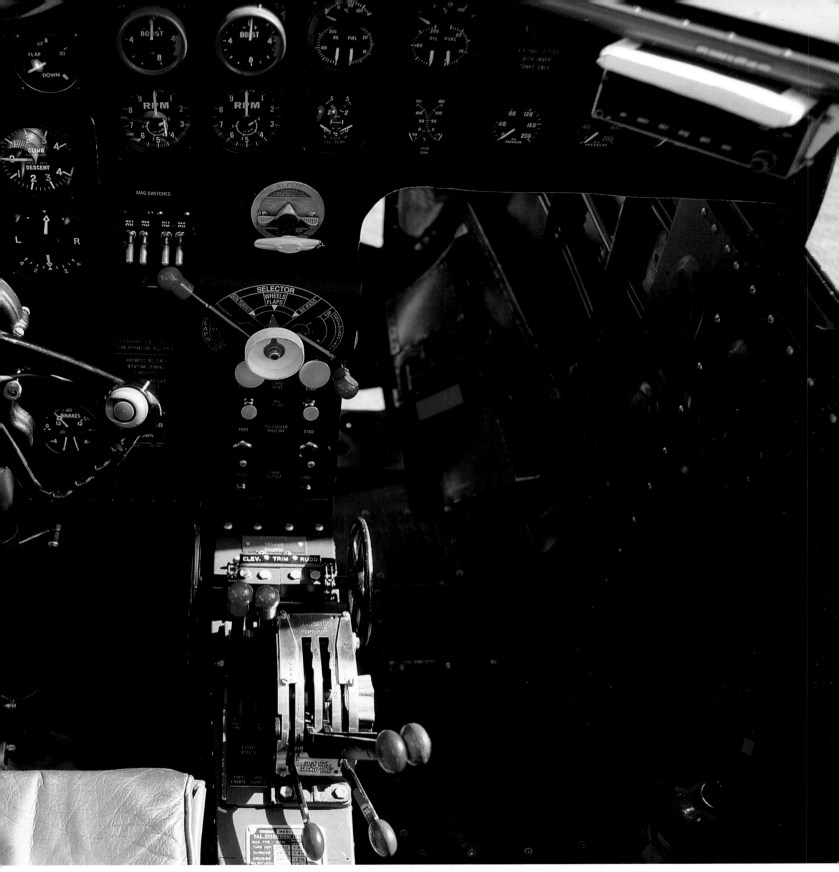

BRISTOL BLENHEIM Mk IV
AIRCRAFT RESTORATION COMPANY, DUXFORD, ENGLAND

1. CONTROL COLUMN
2. GUN BUTTON
3. COMPASS
4. VOR AND GLIDE SLOPE
5. AIR SPEED INDICATOR
6. ARTIFICIAL HORIZON
7. RATE OF CLIMB INDICATOR

8. ALTIMETER
9. DIRECTIONAL GYRO
10. TURN AND BANK INDICATOR
11. BRAKE PRESSURE GAUGE
12. MAG SWITCHES
13. HYDRAULIC CONTROLS
14. PROP PITCH CONTROL

15. THROTTLES
16. MIXTURE CONTROLS
17. TRIM WHEEL
18. CARB HEAT, OIL COOLER SHUT-OFF, CARB CUT-OUT CONTROLS
19. LIFE RAFT RELEASE HANDLE
20. BOOST GAUGES

21. TACHOMETERS
22. FUEL AND OIL TEMP GAUGES
23. CARBURETTOR TEMP GAUGE
24. OIL PRESSURE GAUGE
25. OIL PRESSURE GAUGE
26. FLAP INDICATOR
27. AIR BRAKE CONTROL
28. CYLINDER HEAD TEMP GAUGE

BEAUFIGHTER

IMMENSELY STRONG, WITH A MUSCLE-BOUND LOOK,
THE BEAUFIGHTER PROVED TO BE EVERY INCH A THOROUGHBRED.

The defeat of the German Luftwaffe in the summer and autumn of 1940 did not end the Battle of Britain. Although the daylight skies may have been cleared of German aircraft, the Luftwaffe decided to continue the battle under the cover of darkness. As early as August, Kampfgruppe 100, a special "pathfinder" squadron, used a frightening new electronic device, the X-Gerate, to help find its targets at night. Using incendiary bombs to mark the targets, the follow-on squadrons would dump high explosives into the flames. Beginning on September 7, 1940, 250 German bombers targeted London, dropping 330 tons (300 tonnes) of bombs. For the next 57 nights, London was attacked relentlessly. As the Blitz intensified, the need for an effective night-fighter became paramount. Early night-fighters were hastily converted Blenheim bombers. Fitted with a belly gun pack armed with four 0.303-inch machine guns, the Blenheims proved too slow. Defiants, Hurricanes, and Spitfires were also used to little effect.

It was not until the introduction of the Bristol Beaufighter that the RAF had an aircraft capable of carrying the added weight of the new Mark IV AI (airborne radar) without sacrificing performance. Powered by two Bristol Hercules, and armed with four 20-mm cannons and six 0.303-inch machine guns (four in the starboard wing and two in the port wing), the Beaufighter possessed massive firepower and excellent speed and endurance. Based on the successful Bristol Beaufort torpedo bomber, the Beaufighter was a new design that incorporated the Beaufort's wing, tail, landing gear, and other systems. Because of this, the Beaufighter was quickly put into production. After only six months from the initial

ABOVE: BEAUFIGHTER IVF OF 272 SQUADRON ON THE MOVE AT LUQUA, MALTA.
ABOVE RIGHT: PILOT AND NAVIGATOR POSE WITH THEIR MERLIN-ENGINED BEAUFIGHTER AT GIBRALTAR.

design, the first Beaufighter prototype took to the air. The only shortcomings the Beaufighter displayed were a tendency to swing on take-off and landing and an instability at low speeds. These were corrected in later marks with the addition of a large dorsal fin.

RAF squadrons began receiving the new Beaufighter in September 1940. As the crews (pilot and radar operator) gained experience with their new aircraft and equipment, the number of air-to-air victories began to climb. By the end of the war, John Cunningham, who began flying Beaufighters in 1940, was the second-most-successful night-fighter pilot, with 20 victories.

In late 1941, the Blitz declined to almost nothing. As the Luftwaffe prepared for operation "Barbarossa" in the east, many bomber units were transferred to the Eastern front. With few nocturnal raiders over Britain, Beaufighters were turned to offensive operations. Flying over the waters around Britain, heavily armed Beaufighters attacked airfields on the continent, and shipping and submarines in the North Sea and the Bay of Biscay. In the Mediterranean, Coastal Command made an urgent request for long-range fighters. Beaufighters soon equipped 252 Squadron on Malta. To extend its range, the six wing-mounted machine guns were removed and fuel tanks added. No. 252 Squadron would play a major role in the destruction of enemy shipping and aircraft over North Africa and the Mediterranean.

In North Africa, the Beaufighter operated by night as well as by day. The first American night-fighter squadrons to see action were equipped with the Beaufighter Mk VIF. Four squadrons of the 12th Air Force — 414, 415, 416 and 417 NFS — began operations in the Mediterranean during 1942–43. These units saw extensive service during the German retreat from North Africa and provided effective night air cover during the Anzio and Salerno landings in Italy.

In the Pacific and Burma, RAF and RAAF Beaufighter squadrons racked up an impressive record of enemy aircraft and shipping destroyed. With its heavy armament and rugged construction, the Beaufighter proved to be one of the most effective twin-engine fighter-bombers in the Pacific theatre.

A total of 5,564 Beaufighters were built. The last to serve flew with the RAAF until 1960.

THE PILOT'S
P E R S P E C T I V E

RAYNE SCHULTZ
GROUP CAPTAIN
RCAF (RET.), DFC, OMM, CD

I found the Beaufighter cockpit to be very well designed—a world of improvement over the Blenheim. The view out the front was fabulous, but the interesting thing in the early stages of flying the Beaufighter was landing. The first few landings were quite tricky, because you had nothing to judge with—the nose dropped right off. Before that, flying the Blenheim, you had your nose to work with on the horizon.

One of the things I didn't like about the cockpit was the gunsight. To see forward you could undo the gunsight and move it over to the side. This blocked your view to the side, but not significantly. When it was in front, however, you were guaranteed to bang your forehead when you pranged. The instrumentation was marvellous and all the other controls were easy to hand. The comfort level and heating were also good — a world of difference compared to the Blenheim. Once you strapped in, it was really quite snug.

Getting into the airplane was difficult. You came in from the bottom. The seat would collapse and buckle forward, then you would pull yourself up on two rails along the top of the fuselage. You put your feet in and over and finally pulled the back of the seat forward to the upright position so you could sit. That seat could be a killer. I saw one crew die right in front of my eyes. The mechanism that locked the seat must have worn down. Right after take-off, the seat buckled and forced the pilot into the control column. He went straight into the ground.

In some ways, the Beaufighter cockpit was better than the Mosquito. The view from the cockpit was similar to a single-seat fighter.

BRISTOL BEAUFIGHTER Mk IC
USAF MUSEUM, DAYTON, OHIO

1. CONTROL COLUMN
2. GUN BUTTON
3. BLIND APPROACH VISUAL INDICATOR
4. AIRSPEED INDICATOR
5. ARTIFICIAL HORIZON
6. RATE OF CLIMB INDICATOR
7. OIL PRESSURE GAUGE
8. OIL PRESSURE GAUGE
9. ALTIMETER
10. DIRECTION INDICATOR
11. TURN AND BANK INDICATOR
12. GUNSIGHT
13. RPM INDICATOR (PORT)
14. RPM INDICATOR (STARBOARD)
15. FLOODLIGHT DIMMER SWITCH
16. VENTILATOR
17. COMPASS
18. FIRE-EXTINGUISHER BUTTONS
19. FLOODLIGHT DIMMER SWITCH
20. UNDERCARRIAGE AND TAIL-WHEEL INDICATORS
21. FUEL PRESSURE GAUGES
22. BOOST GAUGE
23. ELEVATOR TRIM TAB CONTROL
24. AILERON TRIM TAB CONTROL
25. THROTTLE QUADRANT
26. AIRSCREW SPEED CONTROLS
27. FUEL COCK CONTROL WHEELS
28. HYDRAULIC EMERGENCY SELECTOR LEVER
29. FLAP CONTROL
30. PILOT'S SEAT (COLLAPSED)
31. UNDERCARRIAGE AND TAIL WHEEL INDICATOR SWITCH
32. CYLINDER HEAD TEMP
33. OXYGEN GAUGES
34. FUEL CONTENTS GAUGE
35. PNEUMATIC SYSTEM PRESSURE GAUGE

NAVIGATOR'S VIEW OF THE BEAUFIGHTER COCKPIT.

de HAVILLAND
MOSQUITO

THE MOSQUITO WAS THE FIRST TRULY SUCCESSFUL MULTI-ROLE
COMBAT AIRCRAFT, CREATING THE MODERN CATEGORY OF THE
HEAVY, LONG-RANGE INTERDICTION/STRIKE FIGHTER.

On November 25, 1940, the first Mosquito prototype completed its maiden flight. Reaction to its performance was immediate. Critics who had called the aircraft a waste of time soon saw it as an instrument of salvation. Although initial scepticism greeted the new bomber, the Mosquito would prove to be one of the most versatile aircraft of the Second World War. The only real problem with the Mosquito was its lack of availability. Serious production began relatively late in the war, and because of its versatility, there were never enough Mosquitoes in its many versions to satisfy demand. It was only after the Battle of Stalingrad and the American victory at Midway that the Mosquito became available in decent numbers.

The key to the Mosquito's success was its external shape and radical wood construction. Aerodynamically, the Mosquito was an extremely clean design. Its small size and neat packaging enabled the designers to wrap the Mosquito around a good-sized bomb bay, which in later versions could carry a bomb load greater than that of the Boeing B-17. But the Mosquito was far from perfect. For pilots unfamiliar with the Mosquito, it was a very demanding machine. Also, because of its wooden construction, belly landings could result in the underside being ripped off, and along with it, the crew's legs. Finally, incendiary anti-aircraft fire would often turn the aircraft into a fiery mass.

The Mosquito's first combat mission of the war occurred on September 17, 1941, when a photo-reconnaissance Mosquito from No. 1 Photo Reconnaissance Unit flew towards the border of Spain and France. The Mosquito's high-speed performance enabled it to avoid most interception attempts; only through careful planning and with determined pilots could the Germans hope to catch the Mosquito. In December 1941, the first photo-reconnaissance Mosquito was lost. Capable of flying farther than the PR version of the Spitfire, the Mosquito always caused the German defences to react with fierce determination.

As a night-fighter, the Mosquito would go on to become the Allies' primary weapon. The first kill was achieved in May 1942, and for the rest of the year, the night-fighter squadrons enjoyed first-delivery priority. But as the nocturnal German threat subsided, the Mosquito took the offensive and adapted the intruder role. To help protect the RAF heavy bombers, Mosquito night-fighters gravitated to known German night-fighter bases and attacked the fighters as they took off and landed.

In the bombing role, the Mosquito would prove to be very successful. Capable of carrying 4,000 pounds (1,814 kg) of bombs (one version with an enlarged bomb bay could carry a single 4,000-pound bomb), Mosquitoes ranged as far as Berlin. During the long winter nights of 1944–45, individual Mosquitoes would bomb Berlin twice in a single night. In the last RAF raid of the war, 125 Mosquitoes attacked Keil and all returned safely.

As a fighter-bomber, the Mosquito gained fame with its celebrated raid on Amiens Prison in February 1940. With pinpoint low-level bombing, Mosquitoes from the 2nd Tactical Air Force breached the walls of the prison and sprang more than 250 prisoners facing execution by the Gestapo.

In the end, the "wooden wonder" could do it all. Never before had one aircraft fufilled so many roles. Designed as a high-speed bomber, the Mosquito soon found itself transformed into an effective reconnaissance aircraft, night-fighter, fighter-bomber, mine-layer, anti-submarine aircraft, and courier plane.

ABOVE: BOMB-CARRYING MOSQUITO FIGHTER-BOMBER ON A DAYLIGHT SORTIE. *RIGHT*: WING COMMANDER JOHN B. SELBY AND HIS OBSERVER LOOKING AT THEIR MOSQUITO II, MALTA, JUNE 1943. *INSET*: LEND-LEASE MOSQUITO MK XVI WITH THE 802 RECONNAISSANCE GROUP.

THE PILOT'S
P E R S P E C T I V E
RAYNE SCHULTZ
GROUP CAPTAIN
RCAF (RET.), DFC, OMM, CD

I flew the Mosquito for well over a thousand hours, and one of the things that they never did fix was the tensioning for the throttles. It was either too tight or too loose. Too loose, your throttles could start coming back as you changed hands to raise your undercarriage on take-off. You could end up in a lot of trouble. The view through the canopy was superb, but it wasn't as good as in the Beaufighter. The compass was down low by your left knee and was difficult to see, but the instrument panel was excellent. The engine instruments were well placed, but the whole throttle quadrant was not very good. The comfort level was about the same as in the Beaufighter, but the heating in the Mosquito was superior to both the Beaufighter and the Blenheim.

Frankly, there's not a lot that I didn't like about the Mosquito. I am prejudiced to this day, and consider it one of the finest airplanes I ever had my hands on.

T H E
NAVIGATOR'S
P E R S P E C T I V E
VERN WILLIAMS
FLIGHT LIEUTENANT,
NAVIGATOR, RCAF, DFC

I flew in the Beaufighter and the Mosquito, but I preferred the Mosquito. I found the Mosquito to be relatively comfortable, but because I looked after the airborne radar, I was too busy to take much notice. I didn't like the navigator's position in the Beaufighter. It was located in the middle of the aircraft, apart from the cockpit. It was cold and drafty, and you didn't know what was going on. You could only talk to the pilot by intercom. In the Mosquito, you sat right beside the pilot, which gave you a ringside seat. I preferred that because I felt more confident and more like a member of the team.

You also felt safer getting out of the Mosquito, with the door right beside you (in the fighter version). In case of emergency, the navigator would be the first one out. That was a comfort. The Mosquito was a great aircraft.

de HAVILLAND MOSQUITO B Mk (thirty-five converted to TT Mk 35)
AEROSPACE MUSEUM, COSFORD, ENGLAND

1. THROTTLES
2. PROPELLER SPEED CONTROL LEVERS
3. FRICTION ADJUSTING KNOBS
4. TAIL TRIM INDICATOR
5. COMPASS
6. OIL PRESSURE GAUGE
7. SUCTION GAUGE
8. RPM INDICATORS
9. OIL TEMP GAUGE
10. OIL PRESSURE GAUGE

11. COOLANT TEMP GAUGE
12. CONTROL COLUMN
13. AIRSPEED INDICATOR
14. ARTIFICIAL HORIZON
15. RATE OF CLIMB INDICATOR
16. ALTIMETER
17. DIRECTION INDICATOR
18. TURN AND BANK INDICATOR
19. FLAPS POSITION INDICATOR
20. UNDERCARRIAGE SELECTOR LEVER (CENTRE), FLAPS SELECTOR LEVER (RIGHT)

21. AILERON TRIM TAB CONTROL/INDICATOR
22. PROPELLER FEATHERING BUTTONS
23. RADIATOR FLAP SWITCHES, NAVIGATION LAMP SWITCH, FUEL PUMP SWITCH, NAVIGATION LIGHT SWITCH, PILOT HEAD SWITCH
24. FUEL CONTENTS GAUGE OUTER TANK

25. EMERGENCY OXYGEN BOTTLES STOWAGE
26. BOMB AIMER ELBOW CUSHION
27. INSTRUMENT LIGHT
28. SEAT ADJUSTMENT HANDLE
29. BRAKE PRESSURE GAUGE
30. DIMMER SWITCH FOR INSTRUMENT AND CHART TABLE FLOODLAMPS

HAWKER
TYPHOON

AS AN INTERCEPTOR THE TYPHOON WAS A FAILURE, BUT AT LOW AND MEDIUM ALTITUDES IT PROVED TO BE AN EXCELLENT FIGHTER AND AN EVEN BETTER GROUND-ATTACK AIRCRAFT.

First conceived in 1937, the Typhoon was designed to succeed the Hawker Hurricane. The Hawker design team was encouraged by the new 24-cylinder, liquid-cooled Sabre engine being developed by the Napier Company. Promising more than 2,000 horsepower, the new Sabre engine was twice as powerful as the Rolls-Royce Merlin in service at the time and would provide a quantum leap in performance. Early flight tests revealed a host of problems. Engine failures were common, and on May 9, 1940, the prototype suffered a partial failure of the monocoque fuselage, just aft of the cockpit. Early armament consisted of twelve 0.303-inch machine guns, but was later changed to four 20-mm cannons.

In September 1941, the Luftwaffe introduced a new and formidable fighter. The introduction of the Fw 190 in many ways saved the Typhoon from extinction. Many in the RAF felt the Typhoon should have been cancelled. The Fw 190 proved superior to the Spitfire Mk V, and when the Germans intensified their low-level "hit-and-run" raids on the English coast, the Spitfire was hard pressed to meet the threat. As a high-altitude fighter, the Typhoon fared poorly, but down low the Typhoon was capable of catching any fighter or bomber the Luftwaffe chose to use.

Compared to other fighters, such as the Spitfire, the Hurricane, and the Mustang I, the Typhoon was an operational nightmare, plagued by engine failures, compressibility, and structural failures. The Typhoon was also the victim of friendly fire, as it closely resembled the Fw 190 and many Allied pilots mistook it as such. It was not until the Typhoon was fitted with two 250-pound (113 kg) bombs and used as a tactical fighter that it came into its own. In 1943, the Typhoon was tested with rocket projectiles and proved a perfect fit. From that point forward, the Typhoon was one of the most effective tactical fighter-bombers of the war.

As the Allies made plans for D-Day, Typhoon squadrons were soon incorporated into the 2nd Tactical Air Force. Shortly after D-Day, priority was given to basing Typhoons on the Continent. As the Allied Armies pushed their way from the beaches, Typhoons kept a steady pressure on the Germans. With Spitfire and Mustang escort, Typhoons armed with bombs and rocket projectiles destroyed vehicles, tanks, ammunition dumps, troop concentrations, and rail transport. The Germans were forced to move men and equipment at

night, severely restricting their ability to fight. In early August 1944, the 7th German Army was trapped in the narrow confines surrounding the town of Falaise. For 12 days, Typhoons from the 2nd Tactical Air Force rained bombs and rockets on the retreating Germans. In the end, the German Army was destroyed, and the battle for France was over. As the Allies pushed into Belgium and Holland, the Typhoon squadrons moved with them. In late September 1944, Typhoons began operating from airfields in Holland. From there, Typhoons would operate over Germany itself. The effectiveness of the Typhoon in the fighter-bomber role is reflected in records of 124 Wing, 2nd Tactical Air Force. From June 6, 1944, to January 1945, its pilots claimed 115 German tanks, 2 armoured cars, and 494 motor vehicles destroyed, as well as 76 tanks, 1 armoured car, and 292 motor vehicles damaged. Typhoon losses were also heavy. Between June 6, 1944, and December 1944, 407 Typhoons were lost. During April 1945, at least 38 Typhoons were lost to flak.

After the war, the Typhoon quickly disappeared. Of the 3,317 Typhoons built, only one survives, at the RAF Museum, in Hendon.

A POSED SHOT OF A TYPHOON FIGHTER-BOMBER, OF 175 SQUADRON IN A BLAST-WALL DISPERSAL POINT AT COLERNE.

THE PILOT'S
PERSPECTIVE
ED MCKAY
FLIGHT LIEUTENANT RCAF (RET.)

U nlike the Spitfire, whose smaller cockpit was entered by stepping down into it from the port wing root, it was quite a climb up the starboard side of the Typhoon! Early cockpit enclosures on the Typhoon consisted of an automobile-style hinged door and roof. This added considerably to the perils of bail-out or forced landing. Later versions were equipped with the standard sliding bubble hood, with improved all-round visibility.

The Typhoon suffered from high levels of carbon monoxide in the cockpit. You had to wear your oxygen mask at all times, from start-up to shutdown. This problem was never solved. Before mandatory oxygen use, the fumes killed a number of pilots.

The roomy cockpit was equipped with the standard British blind flying instrument panel. Surrounding the panel were numerous dials, gauges, and indicators. The circular spade grip on top of the control column housed the brake control and firing button for the four 20-mm cannons. The throttle handle included the bomb and rocket release button. Below that were the controls for the radiator, undercarriage, trims, flaps, etc. It was a very convenient layout.

I found the gradual adjustment of flaps on the Typhoon to be a welcome change from the Spitfire. In the Spitfire, the flaps deployed very quickly and you only had two positions, full up or down. You also had to switch hands in the Spitfire when taking off. The throttle was on the left and the undercarriage control was on the right. In the Typhoon, the throttle and undercarriage controls were grouped together on the left side.

The official pilot's notes for the Typhoon cockpit list 89 controls, dials, indicators, levers, etc. In a normal operational flight you would use about 30 of them. Noise level in the cockpit was high, requiring a snugly fitting helmet. Generally, I found the Typhoon cockpit to be conveniently laid out for visual monitoring, and the controls were easily accessible.

HAWKER TYPHOON Mk IB
RAF MUSEUM, HENDON, ENGLAND

1. CONTROL COLUMN
2. GUN BUTTON
3. CAMERA BUTTON
4. AIRSPEED INDICATOR
5. ARTIFICIAL HORIZON
6. CLIMB INDICATOR
7. DIRECTIONAL GYRO
8. ALTIMETER
9. UNDERCARRIAGE INDICATOR
10. ENGINE STARTER BUTTONS
11. OXYGEN CONTROL PANEL
12. AIR LOUVRE
13. AIR PRESSURE GAUGE
14. FLAP POSITION INDICATOR
15. IGNITION SWITCHES
16. UNDERCARRIAGE LEVER
17. ENGINE START CUT-OUT
18. PITCH LEVER
19. THROTTLE
20. RUDDER PEDAL

ARMOURERS READY A TYPHOON WITH 1,000-POUND BOMBS. NOTE THE THREE-BLADED PROP.

A V R O
LANCASTER

THE LANCASTER WAS THE UNDISPUTED HEAVYWEIGHT CHAMPION OF THE WAR! IT WAS CAPABLE OF CARRYING THE HEAVIEST BOMB LOAD OF ALL FOUR-ENGINE BOMBERS OF THE SECOND WORLD WAR.

Powered by four powerful Rolls-Royce Merlin engines, the Avro Lancaster was a direct descendant of the ill-fated Manchester. The Manchester, which employed two Vultee engines, was terribly unreliable and was detested by its crews. In a move to rectify the problem, Avro lengthened the wing and added two more engines. The re-design was a brilliant stroke, and the Lancaster soon became the workhorse of RAF Bomber Command.

Capable of delivering a large bomb load over a great distance, the Lancaster greatly enhanced Bomber Command's ability to strike deep into Germany.

Introduced in 1942, the Lancaster soon proved to be superior to the Short Stirling and the Handley Page Halifax. The Lancaster cruised at just under 300 miles per hour (483 km/h). The crew consisted of the pilot, flight engineer, navigator/bombardier, wireless operator, and top and tail gunners. Able to withstand considerable battle damage, the Lancaster was easy to build and easy to repair. More than 7,000 were produced by British and Canadian factories. With a long and large bomb bay, the Lancaster could accept 12,000 pounds (5,443 kg) of bombs. Specially modified versions could carry the massive 22,000-pound (9,979 kg) Grand Slam "earthquake" bomb.

A RARE DAYLIGHT PHOTOGRAPH OF THREE LANCASTERS IN FORMATION.

By 1943, Bomber Command could mount raids with nearly 800 aircraft, half of which were Lancasters. The aircraft's most spectacular success involved Lancasters from 617 Squadron—the "Dam Busters" breached the Moehne and Eder Dams in the Ruhr Valley. On the night of May 16, 1943, 19 specially modified Lancasters set out, each fitted with a cylindrical "bouncing bomb." Flying at just 60 feet (18.3 m) above the water, each Lancaster had to maintain the correct altitude in order for the bomb to bounce correctly and hit the target. Originally, three dams were targeted, but only two were breached. Of the 19 Lancasters that took part, two aborted and eight were destroyed. Just two of the 56 men aboard the downed aircraft survived.

One unique feature that set the Lancaster apart from its contemporaries was its massive, uninterrupted, constant-section bomb bay. Originally designed to accept bombs as big as the 4,000-pound (1,815 kg) "cookie," many Lancasters were modified with larger bomb doors to accommodate the 8,000-pound (3,630 kg) or the larger 12,000-pound (5,445 kg) bombs. The Lancaster was blessed with few vices and could be flown very aggressively when the situation required. Using the practised "corkscrew" manoeuvre, many Lancasters managed to escape being shot down by pursuing German night-fighters. The sequence of wing over, maximum-rate descent, and climbing turn stressed the airframe to the maximum. When you consider that the aircraft was loaded with bombs and fuel, this was a truly remarkable feat.

As the bombing campaign grew, the Lancaster was tasked to carry larger and larger bombs. Several German targets were impervious to the usual 500-pound (227 kg) and 1,000-pound (454 kg) bombs. As a result, in 1943, the 12,030-pound (5,457 kg) Tallboy bomb was introduced. Dropped from a good height, the Tallboy would develop a terminal velocity well above the speed of sound and bury itself deep in the ground before exploding. The resulting shock wave would destroy even the heaviest structures. One of the more famous Tallboy operations was the sinking of the German battleship *Tirpitz*. Specially modified Lancasters from 617 Squadron completed the attack, with the loss of one aircraft. In February 1944, the 22,000-pound (9,979 kg) Grand Slam was introduced. Lancasters, again from 617 Squadron, dropped 41 of the bombs on targets including the U-boat pens at Farge, near Bremen.

The last bombings by Lancasters occurred on April 25, 1945, during an operation against submarine fuel stores.

THE PILOT'S
PERSPECTIVE
H. TERRY GOODWIN
FLIGHT LIEUTENANT RCAF (RET.), DFC, DFM

I got my wings two days before Pearl Harbor, flying a Harvard. From Harvards I went to England and learned to fly Oxfords and then Hampdens. I also scrounged some time on Ansons, so I was familiar with what Avro was doing. I flew the Manchester and found that its cockpit was identical to the Lancaster.

The cockpit in the Lancaster used the RAF blind flying panel, so it was very easy for me to move from the British trainers to the Lancaster. Those who didn't train with the blind flying panel found it very difficult to convert to night flying and even found day flying difficult in heavy fog and industrial haze.

The Lancaster cockpit was beautiful. It was originally set up for two pilots, but that was changed before it started operations. Personally, I thought the flap indicator was poorly situated, as the view was blocked when you pushed the throttles all the way forward. That's the only the real concern I had. If it had been over on the left side, where it usually was, it would have been difficult for the flight engineer to see it. On the other hand, I didn't like the flight engineer handling the flaps, because it altered the trim of the aircraft.

The instrument panel, throttles, and landing gear controls were well laid out and quite useful and easy to hand. The cockpit itself was warm and comfortable, and the view through the canopy was very good. There was even a bulge on the side of the canopy where you could see down and towards the back. The Lancaster had no bad habits. It flew much the same as the Anson. In fact, when properly trimmed, the Lancaster practically flew itself.

AVRO LANCASTER Mk VII
Lincolnshire Heritage Centre, East Kirkby, England

1. Autopilot pressure gauge
2. P.4 magnetic compass
3. Control column
4. ASI
5. Artificial horizon
6. Rate of climb indicator
7. Turn and bank indicator
8. DF indicator
9. DR compass repeater
10. Ignition switches
11. Undercarriage indicator switch
12. Engine starter switches
13. Boost gauge: port outer
14. Boost gauge: port inner
15. Boost gauge: starboard inner
16. Boost gauge: starboard outer
17. RPM indicator: port outer
18. RPM indicator: port inner
19. RPM indicator: starboard outer
20. RPM indicator: starboard inner
21. IFF detonator buttons
22. Bomb containers jettison button
23. IFF switch
24. Suction gauge
25. Vacuum change-over cock
26. Oxygen regulator gauges
27. Clock
28. Flap position gauge
29. Supercharger gear change
30. Feathering buttons
31. Fire extinguisher push buttons
32. Triple pressure gauge
33. Signalling switch box
34. Throttles
35. Propeller speed control levers
36. Boost coil switch
37. Starboard Master Engine Cocks

Far Left: Rod cleaning the front machine guns of Lancaster R5666/KM-F, while another member of the ground crew cleans the cockpit windows.

SEVERSKY P-35

LOCKHEED P-38
LIGHTNING

BELL P-39 AIRACOBRA

CURTISS P-40 WARHAWK

REPUBLIC P-47
THUNDERBOLT

CONSOLIDATED
B-24 LIBERATOR

NORTH AMERICAN
B-25 MITCHELL

MARTIN B-26 MARAUDER

BOEING B-29
SUPERFORTRESS

U.S.A.

North American
P-51 Mustang

Bell P-59 Airacomet

Douglas A-20 Havoc

Boeing B-17
Flying Fortress

Grumman Wildcat

Grumman Hellcat

Chance Vought
Corsair

Douglas Dauntless

SEVERSKY
P-35

NICKNAMED THE "FARMINGDALE FLASH,"
THE P-35 WAS THE FIRST SINGLE-SEAT ALL-METAL MONOPLANE FIGHTER
WITH RETRACTABLE LANDING GEAR TO ENTER SERVICE WITH THE USAAC.

A direct precursor to the mighty P-47 Thunderbolt, the P-35 was first ordered by the USAAC in June 1936. After winning out over the Curtiss Hawk Model 75, a contract for 77 production versions of the SEV-1XP prototype was awarded to the Seversky Aircraft Corporation. As the Army Air Corps' first single-seat all-metal monoplane capable of 310 miles per hour (499 km/h) (in later models), the P-35's uniqueness was short lived as war approached. The 1st Pursuit Group, at Selfridge Field, Michigan, was the first unit to be equipped with the P-35. The P-35 was the first fighter to be delivered to the USAAC without camouflage paint. The all-metal finish would remain until the spring of 1941.

Enthusiasm for the new fighter was considerable, even after six crashed during 1938. In combat the P-35's shortcomings were clearly evident. Unstable and under-armed, the P-35 lacked both armour protection and self-sealing fuel tanks. The one thing that the P-35 did possess was extreme range, utilizing a new innovation called "wet wing," in which the inner wing structure was coated with sealant to create one huge fuel tank. The "wet wing," however, proved to be a maintenance nightmare. As the sealant dried out, fuel leaks would occur, which meant that the wing would have to be disassembled and resealed.

In 1939, the Swedish government chose the P-35 as part of its modernization program for the Royal Swedish Air Force. Designated J-9, the new fighter carried a heavier armament of two 0.30-inch and two 0.50-inch machine guns. The engine was increased to 1,050 horsepower. Deliveries of the new fighter began in early 1940, but the second batch of 60 aircraft never made it.

With war imminent, and the need for combat aircraft reached a critical state, the U.S. War Department suspended foreign orders and seized aircraft destined for other nations. The J-9s bound for Sweden became the P-35A. When 45 were rushed to the Philippine Islands, most arrived with Swedish markings! On December 8, 1941, the Japanese struck. The P-35A proved easy prey for the swift and manoeuvrable Japanese fighters. By December 11, only eight P-35As remained operational, but they fought on. On December 24, six attacked the Japanese landing at Lamon Bay. Shortly after, the remaining fighters were ordered to Batann Field. As they approached the airstrip, anxious U.S. gunners mistook the P-35As for Mitsubishi Zeros and shot them down. On January 11, 1942, the last remaining P-35As were ordered to Del Monte. With four other American fighters, they flew the last combat missions in the Philippines.

On the surface, the P-35A's war record does not seem impressive, but by the end of the Philippine Campaign, the 4th Composite Group, with a mixed bag of P-35As, P-40Bs, and P-40Es, had racked up an impressive score. Against a technically superior force, they managed to shoot down about 60 Japanese aircraft. The first American ace of the War, Lieutenant "Buzz" Wagner, achieved his kills aboard the obsolete P-35A. In the end, the entire P-35A force was destroyed, but only a few were actually shot down in air-to-air combat. Most were destroyed on the ground or shot down by friendly fire.

The P-35A (J-9) would serve with the Royal Swedish Air Force throughout the War. In their defence of Stockholm, the J-9s "intercepted" many B-17s and B-24s that were forced to divert to Sweden because of battle damage sustained over Germany. The J-9 would remain in frontline service with the RSAF until 1947 and some were still in use until the mid-1950s.

ABOVE: THE SEVERSKY P-35A WAS THE FIRST AMERICAN FIGHTER WITH RETRACTABLE UNDERCARRIAGE AND ENCLOSED COCKPIT.
LEFT: P-35AS FROM THE 20TH PURSUIT SQUADRON ON PATROL OVER CLARK FIELD, THE PHILIPPINES.

THE PILOT'S
PERSPECTIVE
COLONEL
WALTER COSS
USAF (RET.)

I first flew the P-35 in May 1940 with the 1st Pursuit Group at Selfridge Field and subsequently with the 17th Pursuit Squadron in the Philippines. After all the trainers, it was a great pleasure to lay my hands on one of the best tactical fighters of its day.

Entry into the cockpit was easy, and there was plenty of head and shoulder room. The flight instruments were mounted directly in front of the pilot and the engine instruments were grouped together down below, to the pilot's right. The control stick and rudder pedals were standard and the throttle quadrant was mounted on the left. The internal dimensions of the cockpit and the positioning of the flight and engine controls were such that little stretching or straining was required.

One thing I did find to be an occasional problem was the cowl flap control located on the top right side of the instrument panel. With his right hand the pilot could open or close the engine cowl flaps. Normally this operation was not a problem, but if you were a wingman in formation it could become one. Your normal position in the cockpit is left hand on the throttle, right on the stick. But if you had to adjust those cowl flaps, you were forced to take your left hand off the throttle and switch hands on the stick! The forward and side views through the canopy were excellent; however, vision to the rear was awkward.

In the air, the P-35 was very responsive, but on the ground it was capable of embarrassing any pilot. The P-35 was a short, coupled aircraft—the tail wheel was not very far away from the main wheels. The main wheels themselves were very close together. This combination makes an aircraft prone to ground loop.

It might well be said that the P-35 had a dual character. In the air it was a joy to fly, but on the ground it would bite the unwary pilot.

SEVERSKY P-35A
USAF MUSEUM, DAYTON, OHIO

1. COCKPIT LIGHT
2. CONTROL COLUMN
3. AIRSPEED INDICATOR
4. TURN AND BANK INDICATOR
5. VERTICAL SPEED INDICATOR
6. ALTIMETER
7. GYRO COMPASS
8. MANIFOLD PRESSURE
9. CLOCK
10. VACUUM GAUGE
11. COWL FLAP CONTROL
12. ENGINE PRIMER
13. OXYGEN GAUGE
14. CARBURETTOR TEMP GAUGE
15. TACHOMETER
16. HOLE
17. FUEL PRESSURE GAUGE
18. FUEL GAUGE
19. HYDRAULIC PRESSURE
20. OIL TEMP
21. CYLINDER HEAD TEMP GAUGE
22. RUDDER PEDALS
23. MANIFOLD PRESSURE SWITCH

THE FIRST P-35S TO ENTER SERVICE WENT TO THE 1ST PURSUIT GROUP.

L O C K H E E D   P - 3 8

LIGHTNING

THE P-38 WAS THE MOST SUCCESSFUL AND VERSATILE TWIN-ENGINE SINGLE-SEAT-FIGHTER OF THE SECOND WORLD WAR.

In 1937, the USAAC issued a requirement for a high-altitude interceptor capable of 360 miles per hour (580 km/h) at 20,000 feet (6,095 m). The Lockheed design team soon realized that a single-engine aircraft would never meet the requirements and settled on a radical twin-engine, twin-boom design. The twin-boom configuration afforded many advantages, such as increased accommodation for the engine and the landing gear, and the concentration of superchargers, radiators, and armament in the nose. The biggest advantage was with the pilot, who obtained an excellent all-around view.

On January 27, 1939, seven months before the start of the Second World War, the first prototype took to the air. Two weeks later, it flew across the continent—in just seven hours and two minutes.

As combat reports from Europe reached the States, many recommendations were adapted and incorporated into the P-38. At the time of the Pearl Harbor attack, the USAAC had on strength a total of 47 P-38Cs and P-38Ds. The next production model to come off the assembly line was the P-38E. The E model dispensed with the original 37-mm cannon and standardized the armament at four 0.50-inch machine guns and one 20-mm Hispano cannon.

In February 1942, the first fully combat-worthy P-38 came off the production line. The P-38F obtained a top speed of 395 miles per hour (636 km/h) at 25,000 feet (7620 m).

During 1942–43, 12 squadrons were equipped with the P-38. Most of these were located in the Pacific and the Aleutian Islands. The first P-38s crossed the Atlantic in July and August 1942. The first German aircraft shot down by an American fighter, an Fw 200 Condor, was credited to a P-38E from Iceland.

The next version off the production line was the P-38G. During 1943, it equipped 27 USAAF squadrons in the Pacific theatre. On April 14, 1943, Navy Intelligence learned that Admiral Isoroku Yamamoto would make an inspection tour of forward bases. Code breakers had the admiral's full agenda, and a plan to intercept Yamamoto was prepared. The P-38 Lightning was the only aircraft capable of completing such a mission. It had the longest range of any fighter in the South Pacific. Special long-range fuel tanks were rushed to Guadalcanal, and on April 18, 16 P-38s of the 339th Fighter Squadron took off. After flying over 400 miles (644 km) at low altitude, the Lightnings found their target and shot down Yamamoto's plane, along with several escorting Zeros.

In Europe and the Mediterranean, the P-38 saw constant action. The Germans called it *dergabelschwanzer Teufel* ("the forked-tailed devil"), but against the Luftwaffe's single-seat fighters, the P-38 found it hard to cope. It was hoped that the Lightning would provide the long-range escort needed to complete the strategic bombing campaign against Germany over Northern Europe. Its long range allowed it to reach Berlin, but its cockpit heating was a disaster. In -60° F (-51° C), pilots were too numb to be effective, and morale suffered. Engine failures were also a problem. Soon, the P-38 was nicknamed "the ice wagon." As the buildup of P-47 and P-51 squadrons increased, the P-38 was relegated to ground-attack missions.

On D-Day, June 6, 1944, the P-38 once again took centre stage. Because of its distinctive shape, the Lightning was chosen to provide fighter cover directly over the invasion fleet.

By 1944, 101 squadrons were equipped with the P-38 Lightning. In the Pacific, the Lightning was credited with over 1,800 Japanese aircraft destroyed. Richard Bong, the top American ace, with 40 victories, flew this amazing aircraft.

ABOVE: FACTORY FRESH P-38H, 1943. *RIGHT*: A P-38H HIGH OVER SOUTHERN CALIFORNIA. *INSET*: ENGINE MAINTENANCE.

THE PILOT'S
P E R S P E C T I V E
JEFFREY L. ETHELL
"Flying the P-38 Lightning"
Flight Magazine, August 1997

Once I was settled in the cockpit, I was taken with the vast expanse of airplane around me. Sitting deep within the center gondola and wing, I quickly got the impression of being buried in the machine; this would intensify in flight. The cockpit is just about perfect in size: not too small, not too large and very comfortable. Having memorized the Pilot's Flight Operating Instructions, I was quickly familiar with the cockpit—absolutely mandatory before flying. The layout is a myriad of switches, and the labelling is often hard to read, particularly since most of the switches sit behind the control wheel. I can see why wartime instructors required a blindfold cockpit check before turning people loose.

The most obvious difference from other wartime fighters—other than having two of everything for the engines—is the dual pistol grip control wheel. Putting both hands on this brings a sense of complete authority. I can see why it was so easy to haul the aircraft into tight turns; both biceps are working. The ergonomics of the wheel are also years ahead of their time: the grips are canted inward to the exact position of one's hands when they're relaxed and held out in front of you.

The engine controls sprout from the left pedestal in all directions. The large, red, round throttle knobs are an ideal size for the left hand, completing the sense of total control given by the wheel grips. The fuel-tank selectors are mounted on the floor, one in front of the other, to the left of the seat—left wing fuel forward, right wing fuel aft. This has been the cause of most P-38 accidents in the past 30 years.

The Lightning may have taken a little more time to master, but the options available to the Lightning pilot were impressive.

Jeffrey Ethell died when the P-38 he was flying crashed in June 1997.

LOCKHEED P-38L LIGHTNING
USAF Museum, Dayton, Ohio

1. Throttles
2. Propeller selector switches
3. Control column
4. Mixture controls
5. Coolant shutter controls
6. Prop feathering switch warning lights
7. Prop feathering swtiches
8. Panel light
9. Hydraulic pressure gauge
10. Altimeter
11. Compass indicator
12. Turn and bank indicator
13. landing gear warning light
14. Suction gauge
15. Directional gyro
16. Artificial horizon
17. Dual manifold pressure gauge
18. Dual tachometer
19. Rate of climb indicator
20. Ignition switches
21. Oil, dilution, starter, engage, light, position and landing light switches
22. Automatic coil cooler switches
23. Generator, battery, coolant flap switches
24. Flap contorl lever
25. Propeller controls
26. Radio box

PILOT ENTERS HIS EARLY MODEL P-38.

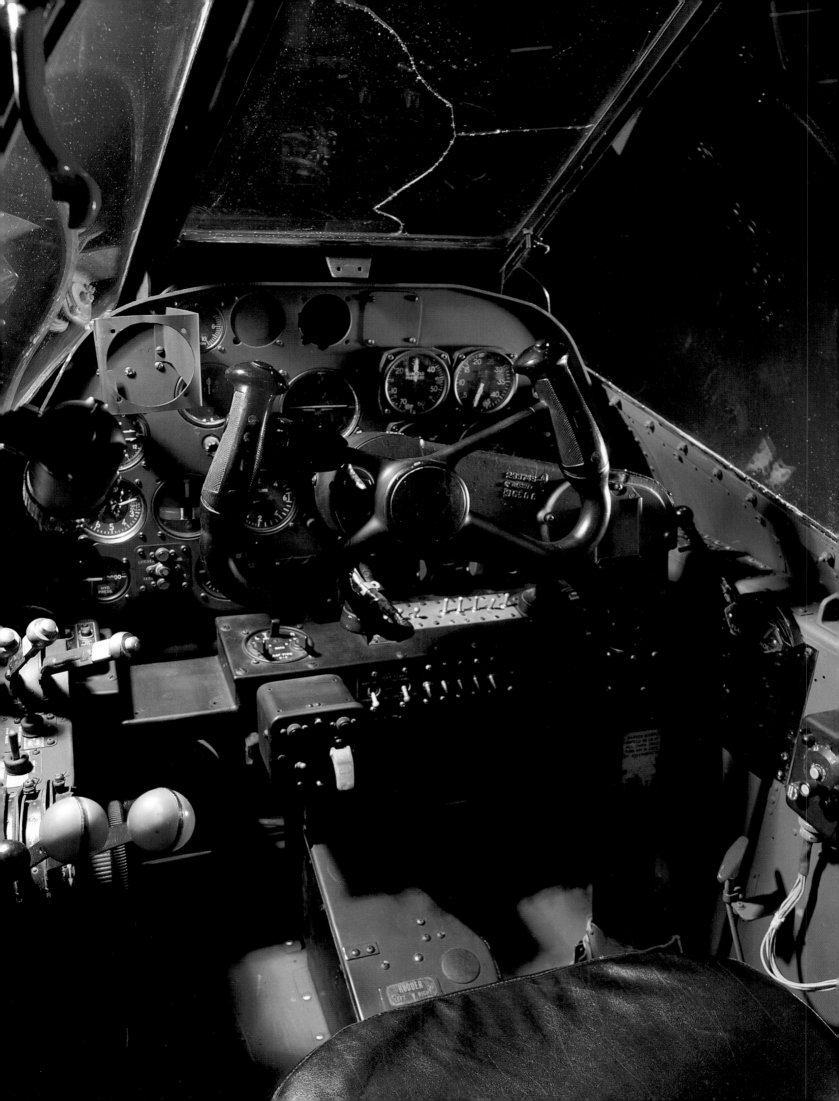

BELL P-39
AIRACOBRA

ITS POOR SPEED AND LOW CEILING WERE MAJOR DEFICIENCIES, BUT IN THE HANDS OF THE RUSSIANS, THE AIRACOBRA WOULD PROVE TO BE A RUGGED AND EFFECTIVE GROUND-ATTACK AIRCRAFT.

On paper, the revolutionary P-39 Airacobra had the look of a winner. On October 7, 1937, the Army ordered a prototype to be built. The XP-39 was a beautiful aircraft with many unique and advanced features. The 1,150-horsepower Allison engine was mounted above the wing and behind the pilot. Located in the centre of gravity, the engine's improved manoeuvrability and the new tricycle landing gear made for easier landings and take-offs. The cockpit, accessed through an automobile-style side door, offered almost perfect all-round visibility. Armament consisted of an impressive 37-mm cannon that fired through the propeller spinner, two fuselage-mounted 0.50-inch machine guns, and four wing-mounted 0.30-inch machine guns. Maximum speed of the prototype was listed at 390 miles per hour (628 km/h).

Based on the XP-39's performance, the British Direct Purchasing Commission ordered 675 examples of the fighter in 1940. Renamed the Caribou I for RAF service, the P-39 proved to be a great disappointment. By the time the Airacobra reached frontline service with the RAF, it was 30 percent heavier and its performance was considerably poorer than advertised. Of the 675 ordered, only four aircraft flew operational sorties, and between them only four missions were completed. Early problems with the compass and poor performance and maintenance problems with the guns led to the Airacobra being taken off operations. The RAF concluded that with the proper improvements the Airacobra would make an excellent day-fighter at altitudes below 20,000 feet (6,096 m) and was well suited to the ground-attack role; however, after the attack on Russia in June 1941, the British decided to divert the bulk of Russia's Airacobra order.

In the opening stages of the Pacific war, the P-39 was pressed into service, to poor results. Its high-altitude performance was miserable, and it proved to be no match for the Mitsubishi Zero.

In the first massive production run of the P-39, 2,095 P-39Ns went to the Soviet Union. There, the Russian pilots found the Airacobra to be a tough and reliable ground-attack aircraft. Its ability to return to base with extensive battle damage made it very popular. In 1942, the 81st and 350th Fighter Groups were equipped with the P-39 and assigned to the Middle East. As part of Operation Torch—the landings in North Africa—the 81st and 350th Fighter Groups flew ground-support missions escorted by Spitfires and P-40s. P-39s also provided convoy protection in the Mediterranean and helped cover the Anzio landings in January 1944.

Although its service in the USAAF was limited, the P-39 served in great numbers with other Allied air forces; its most important role was with the Russian Elite Guard Fighter Squadrons. The P-39Q served along the entire Russian front and saw action during the Battle of Berlin. The Free French Air Force utilized the P-39 in Italy and Southern France, and over 220 Airacobras were supplied to the Italian Co-Belligerent Air Force in 1944. The 332nd Fighter Group became the last American unit to receive the P-39, and in February 1944 they joined the 15th Air Force in Italy.

Total Airacobra production reached 9,558, with the bulk being supplied to the Soviet Union. From its early beginnings, the Airacobra had the look of a winner. Its radical design and advanced features held much promise. In combat, though, it proved to be a liability; however, as the war progressed, the P-39 Airacobra would leave its mark as one of the most effective ground-attack aircraft of the Second World War.

LEFT: TEST PILOT ENTERS P-39 PROTOTYPE. *INSET*: TRAINING FLIGHT OF P-39 AIRACOBRAS.

THE PILOT'S
PERSPECTIVE
GEORGE GUNN
FIRST LIEUTENANT, USAAF

The first time I flew the P-39 was in Victorville, California, in 1944. When I first saw a P-39 I said, "Gosh, that's a small airplane." I didn't think I could get into it. Then, when I was assigned to fly the P-39, I loved it.

The cockpit was very simple. The P-39 had a lot of electrical systems, landing gear, flaps, etc., just like the P-38 and P-40. We had what you called the "blindfold" cockpit check. First you had to sit there and memorize the layout. Then they would blindfold you and ask you where everything was. The P-39 was very easy to get into; just open the door and slide on in. The instrument panel was standard as far as Second World War fighters were concerned. But you had to be careful with the flap switches and landing gear switches, because they were different on each model. The throttle was easy to hand. Of course, it was the largest lever in the cockpit. It was a comfortable cockpit, but after flying the P-39 for three hours you were really hurting. If you had to bail out of the P-39, there was a lever that you pulled. The door would fly off and then you would just roll out the side of the airplane.

The all-round view through the canopy was excellent and you had good visibility when checking your "six." We did a lot of dogfighting with Marine Corsairs stationed in Mojave, and because we took them on below 10,000 feet (3,048 m), we were actually able to outmanoeuvre them. Once, one of the Corsairs had engine trouble and force landed at one of our auxiliary fields. Apparently, the Corsair pilot thought we were flying P-63s because of the way we could outmanoeuvre their Corsairs.

The P-39 was an excellent airplane. Below 10,000 feet (3,048 m), I would have flown it against anything.

P-39Q AIRACOBRA OF THE 53RD FIGHTER GROUP, PANAMA.

BELL P-39Q AIRACOBRA
USAF MUSEUM, DAYTON, OHIO

1. CONTROL COLUMN
2. GUN BUTTON
3. THROTTLE QUADRANT WITH MIXTURE AND PROP CONTROL
4. PILOT HEATER SWITCH, NAVIGATION LIGHT SWITCHES, GENERATOR SWITCH
5. AMMETER
6. GUN CAMERA SWITCH
7. GUN SWITCHES
8. ALTIMETER
9. REMOTE READING COMPASS
10. GYRO COMPASS
11. ARTIFICIAL HORIZON
12. AIRSPEED INDICATOR
13. RATE OF CLIMB INDICATOR
14. TURN AND BANK INDICATOR
15. TACHOMETER
16. COOLANT TEMP GAUGE
17. GEAR BOX PRESSURE GAUGE
18. OIL, FUEL PRESSURE AND TEMP GAUGE
19. MANIFOLD PRESSURE GAUGE
20. SUCTION GAUGE
21. RADIO CONTROL PANEL
22. INGNITION SWITCH
23. THROTTLE FRICTION CONTROL

WARHAWK

"THE P-40 IS THE STRONGEST SHIP IN THE WORLD.
IT'S HEAVY AS HELL, BUT THAT MAKES IT OUT-DIVE JUST ABOUT ANYTHING,
AND IT'LL OUT-DIVE THE JAPANESE TWO TO ONE."
— JOHN VADER, *PACIFIC HAWK*

Like the Hawker Hurricane, the P-40 would prove to be one of the most useful fighters at the start of the Second World War. A supreme workhorse, the P-40 Warhawk would serve on almost every front. Although its exploits never received the same glamorous publicity as the Spitfire or the Mustang, the P-40's contribution to early Allied victories in the air against the Germans, Italians, and Japanese was immense. The first Japanese aircraft to be shot down in the Pacific fell to the guns of the P-40B. This occurred during the attack on Pearl Harbor, when a handful of P-36As and P-40Bs shot down seven Japanese planes. The first Japanese aircraft to be shot down over the Philippines also fell to a P-40B.

The prewar design of the P-40 precluded good high-altitude performance. The P-40 was most effective at heights below 15,000 feet (7,620 m). Although somewhat outdated compared to the Mitsubishi Zero and Messerschmitt Bf 109, the P-40 proved to be a rugged aircraft capable of taking heavy punishment and operating from rough, unprepared airfields. Whatever it lacked in speed and manoeuvrability, the Warhawk made up for in structural rigidity and armament.

At the beginning of 1942, the Allies had little to show for their efforts. Disaster followed disaster, but in the skies above Rangoon, American P-40 pilots were winning battles. The legend of the Flying Tigers is well known. During its 30 weeks of combat, the American Volunteer Group was officially credited with 297 Japanese aircraft destroyed. Using the P-40's superior diving speed and heavy armament, the Americans were able to utilize the Warhawk's best characteristics to great advantage.

In North Africa and Italy, the P-40 (named "Kittyhawk" by the British) proved to be a rugged and worthy opponent. With a top speed of 354 miles per hour (570 km/h) — roughly the same as the Spitfire VC with tropical filter — the Warhawk filled many roles, including interceptor, fighter-bomber, and escort-fighter. Armed with 250-pound (113 kg) and 500-pound (227 kg) bombs, along with six 0.50-inch machine guns, the P-40 became a very effective ground-attack aircraft.

The most severe climate conditions under which the P-40 would operate were in Alaska and the Aleutians. A clear day in either area was a rare occurrence, and operations were severely limited. After the Japanese had set up observation posts on Kiska and Attu in June 1942, the Americans retaliated in August. P-40s and P-39s patrolled unopposed, and as the Allied forces built up, Canadian Warhawks joined the bombers in attacks against Kiska. In May 1943, the Japanese were driven from their outposts, and the P-40 proved that it could operate in the Arctic cold as well as in the desert heat.

The P-40 Warhawk served on almost every front during the Second World War. It was used by the RAF, RAAF, RCAF, RNZAF, SAAF, and USAAF. It was also supplied to the Soviet Union, China, and Brazil. By 1943, its performance was clearly inferior compared to the P-38, P-47, and P-51, but production continued well into 1944.

Like the Hawker Hurricane, the P-40 Warhawk became a true workhorse. Its victories were due in large part to the courageous pilots who flew it. Under the most arduous conditions and against superior fighters, the P-40 managed to win more battles than it lost. In the end, over 16,000 Warhawks were built.

ABOVE: P-40E OF THE "ALEUTIAN TIGERS." *RIGHT*: AVG 3RD SQUADRON "HELLS ANGELS," FLY ALONG THE CHINA–BURMA BORDER, MAY 28, 1942. *INSET*: A DRAMATIC SHOT OF A PILOT ENTERING HIS P-40.

THE PILOT'S
P E R S P E C T I V E
NORM DAWBER
FLYING OFFICER RCAF (RET.)

I flew P-40Es and Fs in Alaska. The P-40 was a lovely airplane. It was built like a Cadillac. It was very heavy, a little over 12,000 pounds (5,443 kg), but the engine was only 1,150 horsepower, which was not really powerful enough. The P-40 should have had at least 1,600 horsepower for good performance, although it did very well in the Middle East.

When you sat in the cockpit you were basically sitting on the floor with your legs almost straight out in front of you. The shelves on each side were several inches wide, allowing you to rest your arms on long flights. The cockpit was evidently designed with the pilot's comfort and convenience in mind. The P-40 was the only aircraft I flew where you had a switch on the left-hand shelf above the throttle, allowing you to trim the ailerons electrically while in flight. It was just another added feature that made it an easy aircraft to fly "hands off" when you had the trim properly set.

Everything in the cockpit was controlled electrically—flaps, landing gear, constant speed propeller, and many other instruments. Down on the right-hand side of the instrument panel there were about 10 breaker switches, which allowed you to reset any of the electrical systems if they became overloaded.

The P-40 had a very roomy cockpit; everything was within easy reach, and with your legs stretched out in front of you it was comfortable even on long flights. The instrumentation was beautifully laid out and the view through the canopy was good. Overall, it was beautiful to fly and great for aerobatics.

P-40 OF THE 23RD FIGHTER GROUP, CHINA.

CURTISS P-40E WARHAWK
USAF MUSEUM, DAYTON, OHIO

1. GUNSIGHT
2. TURN INDICATOR
3. ARTIFICIAL HORIZON
4. LANDING GEAR WARNING LIGHT
5. FUEL SIGNAL WARNING LIGHT
6. FUSELAGE FUEL TANK GAUGE
7. AIRSPEED INDICATOR
8. TURN AND BANK INDICATOR
9. RATE OF CLIMB INDICATOR
10. MANIFOLD PRESSURE GAUGE
11. COOLANT WARNING LIGHT
12. SUCTION GAUGE
13. COOLANT TEMP GAUGE
14. GEAR AND FLAP POSITION INDICATOR
15. CLOCK
16. ALTIMETER
17. TACHOMETER
18. ENGINE GAUGE UNIT
19. ELECTRIC CONTROL PANEL
20. THROTTLE
21. ENGINE PRIMER
22. WINDSCREEN DEFROSTER PUMP
23. GUN BUTTON/ CONTROL COLUMN
24. CANOPY HANDLE
25. AUXILIARY HYDRAULIC HAND PUMP
26. CIRCUIT BREAKERS
27. COMPASS
28. AMP METER
29. CYLINDER PRESSURE GUAGE

THUNDERBOLT

AFFECTIONATELY KNOWN AS THE "JUG," SHORT FOR JUGGERNAUT, THE P-47 THUNDERBOLT WAS ONE OF THE HEAVIEST, MOST POWERFUL SINGLE-SEAT FIGHTERS TO SEE SERVICE WITH THE USAAF.

Produced in greater numbers than any other American fighter, the P-47 proved itself to be one of the most useful Allied fighters in all theatres. According to the USAAF's Office of Statistical Control, the P-47 Thunderbolt completed 545,575 combat sorties in just two and a half years of operational service. In that time, they dropped 132,482 tons (120,188 tonnes) of bombs, fired 59,567 rockets, and used 134.9 million rounds of 0.50-inch machine gun ammunition. P-47s claimed 7,067 enemy aircraft destroyed, including 3,752 in the air and 3,315 on the ground.

Designed around the 18-cylinder R-2800 Double Wasp engine, the P-47 required an enormous propeller to take advantage of this massive powerplant. Exceptionally long landing gear was necessary to keep the propeller tips from hitting the ground during take-off. The landing gear also had to fit into the wings when it was retracted. To make this work, Republic engineers designed a system in which the main gears were shortened by 9 inches (223 cm) on retraction. Armament consisted of eight 0.50-inch Browning machine guns with 350 rounds each. Internal fuel capacity consisted of a main tank and auxiliary tank of 205 and 100 gallons (776 l and 379 l) respectively. Compared to other fighters, the P-47's roomy cockpit was well equipped, packed with the latest systems and devices, such as electric fuel contents transmitters, anti-icing, cabin air-conditioning, and gun-bay heating.

After eight months of design and construction, the XP-47B prototype first flew on May 6, 1941. Deliveries soon followed. The first P-47Cs went to the 56th Fighter Group, and the first escort mission was flown on April 13, 1943. Using 305-gallon (1,155 l) drop tanks, the P-47s could not accompany the bombers all the way to the target and were forced to turn back. Early encounters with seasoned Fw 190A and Bf 109G pilots proved to be an unnerving experience. The P-47 could easily out-dive its opponents, but that was not the object of the exercise. Destroying the Luftwaffe in the air was.

P-47 pilots worried about the fighter's ability to hold its own against the Fw 190. Using a captured Fw 190A-4, a mock combat was flown against a P-47C. At altitudes below 15,000 feet (4,575 m) the Fw 190 had the advantage, but above 15,000 feet the P-47 was faster than both the Fw 190A and Bf 109G. Its heavy armament was devastating, and the P-47 could break combat at will with its tremendous diving ability. The only serious deficiency was the Thunderbolt's range. In mid-1943, the improved P-47D began to replace the C models. Range was also increased with the introduction of two new drop tanks. Developed in the U.S., the teardrop shaped tank had a capacity of 75 gallons (2,841 l); the British tank, of reinforced paper construction, could hold 108 gallons (4,091 l). Now the P-47 could escort its bomber charges deep into Germany. As D-Day approached, and with the introduction of the P-51 Mustang, the P-47s were free to undertake their second operational role — that of ground attack. With the ability to carry two 1,000-pound (454 kg) bombs on the wings as well as the fuselage, the P-47 became the premier ground-attack fighter of the war.

As well as operating in Europe, Thunderbolts also served with the 12th Air Force in the Mediterranean. There they flew bomber-escort and ground-attack missions to great effect. In the Pacific, the P-47 saw action in New Guinea, the Philippines, Saipan, Tinian, Guam, Okinawa, and the China–Burma–India theatre (with the RAF).

Francis S. Gabreski, the third-highest-scoring American ace, tallied 31 kills while flying the P-47 with the 56th Fighter Group.

RIGHT: ASSISTED BY HIS CREW CHIEF, A PILOT ENTERS HIS P-47.
INSET: A P-47 FROM THE 78TH FIGHTER GROUP FLIES HIGH ABOVE THE CLOUDS.

THE PILOT'S
PERSPECTIVE
STEPHEN GREY
THE FIGHTER COLLECTION

The Thunderbolt was equipped with the "grand ballroom" of cockpits. The Eagle Squadron pilots, who converted from Spitfires, found it particularly spacious.

Basically this was a big, robust cockpit designed for big, robust guys. On the left-hand side of the seat was a massive reduction gear box with elevator trim in the vertical plane, rudder trim, and aileron trim in the horizontal plane. Above that was a flap actuator and a big gear lever. The throttle quadrant is typically U.S. Air Force. You have mix to the front, prop next to that, supercharger, and then throttle lever. The throttle lever, by the time the D model "Jugs" were out, had a rotating handle for actually changing the scale on your gunsight. This innovation came from Royal Air Force experiences in the earlier parts of the War.

The main instrument panel on the Thunderbolt was also typical of fighter panels of USAF aircraft. You had all the engine instruments, as well as your altitude and navigation instruments, in the bit that shakes.

The P-47 also had interesting rudder pedals, which you could fold down on a long trip so that you could stretch your feet. Of course, if you got bounced your feet would be in the wrong place!

The view from the cockpit was fine, considering that you had a big, round engine in front of you. The P-47 looks like a large ungainly airplane, but among American Second World War fighters, it was probably one of the more manoeuvrable. In terms of flying, the ailerons were crisp, the rudder was powerful, and the elevator relatively light—much lighter than the Mustang's.

REPUBLIC P-47D THUNDERBOLT
BUTCH SCHROEDER, DANVILLE, ILLINOIS

1. K-14A GUNSIGHT
2. CLOCK
3. AIR SPEED INDICATOR
4. TURN INDICATOR
5. ARTIFICIAL HORIZON
6. CARBURETTOR AIR TEMP GAUGE
7. TURBO RPM GAUGE
8. AMMETER
9. ALTIMETER
10. TURN AND BANK INDICATOR
11. RATE OF CLIMB INDICATOR
12. COMPASS
13. MANIFOLD PRESSURE GAUGE
14. TACHOMETER
15. OIL & FUEL PRESSURE TEMP GAUGE
16. DEFROSTER
17. ENGINE PRIMER
18. IGNITION SWITCH
19. ACCELEROMETER
20. SUCTION GAUGE
21. ENGINE HOURS GAUGE
22. FUEL CONTENTS GAUGE
23. OIL TEMP GAUGE
24. COWL FLAP CONTROL
25. CONTROL COLUMN
26. THROTTLE
27. BOMB/TANK SELECTOR
28. HYDRAULIC PRESSURE GAUGE
29. RECOGNITION LIGHT SWITCHES
30. BOMB/TANK RELEASE

PAT FROM THE 63RD FIGHTER SQUADRON WARMS UP FOR A MISSION IN 1944.

MUSTANG

CONSIDERED BY MANY TO BE THE FINEST AMERICAN FIGHTER OF ALL TIME, THE P-51 MUSTANG WOULD PROVE ESSENTIAL TO ALLIED VICTORY.

In 1940, the North American Aircraft Company was contacted by the British Purchasing Commission. The British were considering North American as a new supplier for the Curtiss P-40, but company designers Raymond Rice and Edgar Schmued saw this as a chance to design a completely new fighter. The British agreed, but the new fighter would have to be completed within 120 days. Incredibly, the new fighter was conceived, designed, and constructed in just 102 days! The NA-73X prototype embodied many new and innovative construction techniques. The engine coolant section was placed behind and below the pilot. The distinctive air-scoop reduced drag. This, coupled with the advanced laminar-flow wing, enabled the big fighter to reach a speed of 382 miles per hour (615 km/h). The British gave it the name Mustang and ordered 320.

In the RAF, the Allison-engine Mustang I was assigned to Army Cooperation Squadrons and used in the low-level reconnaissance role, with ground attack as secondary. Below 15,000 feet (4,575 m), the Mustang was superb and proved to be 25 to 45 miles per hour (40 to 72 km/h) faster than the Spitfire V. Its success was immediate, and on May 10, 1942, the first mission was flown, as Mustangs from 26 Squadron were used to strafe aircraft hangars at Berck sur Mer, in France. The first Mustang kill of the war was credited to an American volunteer flying with the Royal Canadian Air Force during the ill-fated Dieppe raid on August 10, 1942. By 1942, Mustang Is equipped 10 RAF squadrons, 3 Canadian squadrons, and 1 Polish squadron.

As good as the Mustang was, its performance above 15,000 feet (4,575 m) fell off rapidly. Rolls-Royce proposed fitting the Mustang with the proven Merlin engine, and four examples were re-engined and equipped with four-blade propellers. The increase in performances was dramatic. Speed exceeded 400 miles per hour (644 km/h), and with the supercharged Merlin, high-altitude performance was guaranteed.

As 1943 unfolded, the 8th Air Force's attempts to bomb targets deep within Germany were met with tremendous losses. The long range escort provided by the P-47 and P-38 was limited, and in order to reach the vital targets inside Germany, a new escort fighter had to be found. The new P-51B and C models, powered by the Packard Merlin, soon proved themselves to be ideal for long-range escort. Later, when modified with a 75-gallon (322 l) rear fuselage tank, and equipped with two 108-gallon (409 l) drop tanks, the Mustang could reach Berlin and beyond. In 1944, the ultimate D model was introduced, incorporating the bubble canopy with its excellent all-round view; it was also up-gunned to six 0.50-inch machine guns. Powered by the 1,590-horsepower Packard Merlin, the P-51D was in a class by itself. Using its great range, the P-51 was able to take the fight to the enemy and was credited with destroying more enemy aircraft than any other American fighter in Europe.

In the RAF, the Mustang was also used for long-range escort. German naval operations from occupied Norway were a constant threat to Allied shipping. Between 50 and 100 Bf 109s and Fw 190s were stationed in Norway and their actions took a heavy toll on Coastal Command aircraft. Soon, RAF Mustangs provided escort for Beaufighter and Mosquito anti-shipping strikes. While the Americans flew at high altitudes, the Mustangs operating with Coastal Command skimmed the wave tops to avoid enemy radar; round trips of 1,000 miles were common. This type of low-level flying was extremely demanding and is a testament to the quality of the men and the aircraft they flew.

In the end, about 40 USAAF fighter groups and 31 RAF and RCAF Squadrons were equipped with the type.

ABOVE: THREE P-51Ds AND ONE B ON ESCORT MISSION OVER FRANCE, JULY 1944.
RIGHT: WITH HIS CREW CHIEF STANDING BY, A PILOT ENTERS HIS P-51D.

THE PILOT'S
P E R S P E C T I V E
STEPHEN GREY
THE FIGHTER COLLECTION

This airplane is not exactly characteristic of the average American fighter in its internal cockpit size. It's much more European (my shoulders fit against the cockpit wall). The P-51 Mustang had the benefit of a lot of specification input from pilots who were actually fighting when this airplane was designed. I think the layout, compared to other Second World War airplanes, was the most ergonomic.

The flap lever was set low, just right for combat. Above that, the throttle had a classic American design, but you have an extra feature with the stick. If you push the stick forward on the ground you unlock the tail wheel so you can freely rotate. Basically, you end up taxiing the Mustang in confined spaces with the stick forward, which is a little uncanny. On the other hand, the airplane is very stable on the ground with its big wide-track landing gear. If you want to taxi in a straight line and you have a wind problem, you pull the stick all the way back to engage the tail wheel lock and just taxi about 20 degrees to each side of centre. I imagine it would have been a little unusual for the pilot converting from a Spitfire with a freely rotating tail wheel.

The Mustang has a pretty standard and complete instrument panel, excepting that the majority of the instruments are in the principal panel, so you've got altimeter, airspeed indicator, artificial horizon, and engine instruments on the right, all in the panel (the centre bit that shakes about).

Personally, I like to be tightly strapped in an airplane, so that when you roll it your body doesn't rattle around. I guess it's psychological. I don't feel uncomfortable in the bigger cockpits. I just feel more comfortable in the tight cockpits, such as the P-51 Mustang, the Spitfire, or the Bearcat.

MUSTANG ACE COL. DONALD J. BLAKESLEE IN THE COCKPIT OF HIS P-51.

NORTH AMERICAN
P-51-F6D MUSTANG
BUTCH SCHROEDER,
DANVILLE, ILLINOIS

1. K-14A GUNSIGHT
2. SUCTION GAUGE
3. DIRECTIONAL GYRO
4. ARTIFICIAL HORIZON
5. COOLANT TEMP
6. TACHOMETER
7. TURN AND BANK INDICATOR
8. RATE OF CLIMB INDICATOR
9. VOR
10. CARBURETTOR AIR TEMP
11. FUEL OIL PRESSURE GAUGE
12. EMERGENCY CANOPY RELEASE HANDLE
13. OXYGEN REGULATOR
14. LANDING GEAR WARNING LIGHTS
15. IGNITION SWITCH
16. CONTROL COLUMN
17. OXYGEN FLOW BLINKER
18. OXYGEN PRESSURE GAUGE
19. THROTTLE
20. FUEL SELECTOR VALVE
21. FUEL SHUT-OFF VALVE
22. FLUORESCENT LIGHT SWITCH
23. AMMETER
24. CANOPY CRANK AND LOCK HANDLE
25. ELECTRICAL CONTROL PANEL
26. BC-438 CONTROL BOX
27. INSTRUMENT LIGHT

BELL P-59

AIRACOMET

As a fighter, the P-59 was a failure. As America's first jet it was an unqualified success.

On October 1, 1942, the United States entered the jet age. In a tentative flight, the XP-59A obtained a height of just 25 feet (7.6 m). Other flights followed, and on October 2, 10,000 feet (3,048 m) was reached. As the tests continued, it was soon realized that the P-59 was not in the same class as the German Me 262 or Gloster Meteor.

In April 1941, General H. Arnold, Chief of the Army Air Force, witnessed the Whittle engine under test and saw the Gloster Whittle E.28/39 (Britain's first jet airplane) for the first time. Returning to the States, General Arnold soon put in motion the negotiations that would allow General Electric to build and develop the Whittle-designed turbojet. On September 4, 1941, the decision was made to build 15 engines and 3 airframes.

The manufacturer chosen to build the airframes was the Bell Aircraft Company. Bell was chosen for a number of reasons: its factories were less overloaded compared to the other fighter manufacturers, it was close to GE, and the imaginative engineering staff at Bell was well respected. The main goals of the project were to investigate jet propulsion and to determine whether the jet engine was suitable for fighters. Bell's approach was to design a straightforward mid-wing monoplane, with engines fitted in nacelles beneath the wing roots and flush against the sides of the fuselage.

Construction of the prototype began in January 1942. After some delays, the airframe was packed into crates and shipped to Muroc, California, on September 12. Test flights began on October 1, and in the next two

BELOW: THE P-59 WAS AMERICA'S FIRST JET AIRCRAFT.
ABOVE RIGHT: THE P-59B VERSION OF THE AIRACOMET HAD SHORTER WINGS AND TAIL FIN.

days eight flights were completed.

On March 26, 1943, the USAAF ordered a batch of 13 YP-59As for service tests. Using the improved General Electric I-61 turbojet, with a rating of 1,650 lb st (748 kgp), the YP-59A obtained a top speed of 409 miles per hour (658 km/h) at 35,000 feet (10,668 m). It was at this time that the USAAF adopted the name "Airacomet" for its new fighter.

To assess the tactical survivability of the P-59, three Airacomets were flown in mock combat against the P-47D and P-38J Lightning. Outclassed by both aircraft, the USAAF concluded that the P-59 was not "operationally or tactically suited for combat" but would be "an excellent aircraft for research on jet power plants and pressure cabins."

Gunnery trails also revealed the P-59 to have poor directional stability at speeds above 240 miles per hour (547 km/h), making it a poor gun platform. Full-scale production of the P-59 was confirmed on March 11, 1944, when the USAAF ordered 100 P-59As. Deliveries began toward the end of 1944, but the USAAF decided that the P-59 was not an improvement over the piston-engine fighter. An order to cancel was issued, but because it would have been more expensive to cancel than complete the airframes, 20 P-59As and 30 P-59Bs were completed.

The USAAF's first jetfighter group was the 412th of the Fourth Air Force. The P-59 was in service for just over a year and saw no active service or combat deployment.

To a large extent, the Bell P-59 Airacomet was unsuccessful in the fighter role. Its claim to fame came in a less glamorous role. As an airframe test bed for the new jet engine, the Airacomet achieved top marks. Pilots and mechanics cut their teeth on the P-59 and soon graduated to jetfighters with much higher performance. The highest speed achieved by the P-59 was 425 miles per hour (684 km/h).

Impressive as that was, it still was not good enough. It would be the next generation that would soon show the promise of the jet combat aircraft.

THE PILOT'S
P E R S P E C T I V E
COLONEL
KEN CHILSTROM
USAF (RET.)

I was in fighter test for eight years at Wright Field and I flew 147 different military airplanes, including both German and Japanese aircraft. I first flew the P-59 in 1944. The P-59 cockpit was a simple, rudimentary affair and no problem whatsoever to fly.

It was very comfortable, roomy and easy to get into, with plenty of head and shoulder room. The instrument panel was conventional, if somewhat sparse, but was comparable to the piston-engine aircraft of the time. Of course, it took them a few years before they invented the all-attitude gyros that were more suited to jet aircraft. This limited the P-59 and it was restricted to Visual Flight Rules flying. The throttle was in a good position; on the early jet engines you had to ease the throttle open to add more thrust. The all-round view through canopy was excellent. I initially flew the YP model, which didn't have a gunsight, so my view forward was unobstructed. Compared to the Me 262, the P-59 cockpit was much better. The Me 262 cockpit was smaller and less comfortable, and the engine instrumentation was not as good. Of course, the Me 262 was a much faster airplane. It flew at around 0.84 mach. The P-59 didn't even come close to that.

We all thought the P-59 handled a bit like a "kiddy car." The wide landing gear and good visibility made the P-59 very easy to handle, and there was nothing unusual for the pilot to consider.

Jet engines in those days were low on thrust, and they remained that way for a number of years. With the switch to jet engines, the noise in the cockpit was lessened considerably.

As a fighter, the P-59 never succeeded. You have to remember the P-59 was the first American attempt to mate the jet engine with an airframe. Considering that, it was quite good.

BELL P-59B AIRACOMET
USAF MUSEUM, DAYTON, OHIO

1. CONTROL COLUMN	**10.** LEFT ENGINE FUEL SELECTOR SWITCH	**20.** FUEL PRESSURE GAUGE
2. CABIN HEAT	**11.** RIGHT ENGINE FUEL SELECTOR SWITCH	**21.** ALTIMETER
3. HATCH EMERGENCY RELEASE HANDLE	**12.** GUNSIGHT SWITCH	**22.** TURN AND BANK INDICATOR
4. THROTTLE	**13.** FLAP SWITCH	**23.** VSI
5. MIXTURE CONTROL	**14.** ASI	**24.** TACHOMETER
6. LANDING GEAR CONTROL	**15.** CLOCK	**25.** DIRECTIONAL GYRO
7. COCKPIT LIGHT SWITCHES	**16.** RADIO COMPASS	**26.** CANOPY HANDLE CRANK
8. GENERATOR SWITCHES	**17.** ARTIFICIAL HORIZON	**27.** RUDDER PEDAL
9. AMMETER	**18.** ALTIMETER	
	19. ENGINE TEMP GAUGE	

YP-59 AT WRIGHT FIELD.

D O U G L A S   A - 2 0
HAVOC

AT LOW LEVEL, THE A-20 WAS DEVASTATING.
THE COMBINATION OF CONCENTRATED FIREPOWER, SPEED,
AND MANOEUVRABILITY MADE IT THE IDEAL WEAPON FOR PINPOINT ATTACKS.

In the 1930s, many conflicts were in progress around the globe. Japan invaded Manchuria, then China; Italy expanded its Empire into Ethiopia; Spain was in a vicious Civil War; and Germany began to re-arm. The possibility of a second world war seemed very real. Many in the United States chose to ignore world events and concentrate on domestic issues; however, there were those in industry and the military who saw war as a very real possibility. The Douglas Aircraft Company was one such company. In 1936, in anticipation of an Army Air Corps requirement for a light attack bomber, Douglas began development of a twin-engine aircraft.

The prototype DB-7 first flew on October 26, 1938. The new aircraft was exceptionally fast and manoeuvrable and exhibited no serious handling flaws. As impressive as the prototype was, the American government did not order any models. Instead, it was the French Purchasing Company that put the DB-7 into production. The first order of 100 was soon followed by 270 more. Few of the aircraft reached the French before the fall of France in spring 1940. The bulk of the order was taken up by the British and the aircraft renamed "Boston." The United States finally ordered the aircraft in June 1939 and designated it the A-20.

The RAF soon realized that the early Boston was not suited as a day bomber, and many were converted to intruders and night-fighters and designated the "Havoc." The night-fighter Havocs were fitted with the British AI Mk IV radar along with four 0.303-inch machine guns. In the summer of 1942, flying Boston IIIs, the RAF began low-level daylight bombing operations against German targets in France and the low countries. The reputation of the A-20 soon grew, as it proved to be a rugged, capable aircraft, able to take extensive battle damage and return to base.

In the Pacific, the introduction of the A-20 to the War occurred during the attack on Pearl Harbor. Several months later, the 89th Bomber Squadron began operations in New Guinea. Aircraft were soon modified in the field to carry four 0.50-inch machine guns in the nose. Low-level attacks against Japanese ships and airfields proved devastating, and the first A-20 "gunship" was born.

Flying at low level through enemy flak is an extremely hazardous undertaking. But, as one pilot described it, the A-20's low-level flight characteristics were "sensational." Visibility from the cockpit was excellent and the instruments, hydraulics, and electrical systems were considered very good. The A-20 had the feel of a single-seat fighter, with a top speed of around 335 miles per hour (539 km/h).

Back in Europe, the buildup of tactical aircraft for the invasion of Europe was in full swing. Three bomb groups were equipped with the A-20 and assigned to the 9th Air Force. Early low-level attacks suffered heavy losses, and the A-20s were forced to change tactics. In the Pacific, the A-20's low-level tactics proved to be decisive. The A-20's forward firepower, speed, and manoeuvrability made it the ideal weapon. Japanese convoys were a favourite target, and during the Battle of the Bismarck Sea an entire convoy was annihilated.

A-20 production reached 7,385, of which 3,125 went to Russia. There they were used in many different roles, including low-level strafing and torpedo bombing. After the war, most of the A-20s were declared surplus and melted down.

LEFT: PILOT CLIMBING INTO A-20C BOMBER. *ABOVE*: A BOSTON III ON TAKE-OFF FROM MT. FARM IN 1944.

THE PILOT'S
P E R S P E C T I V E
COLONEL
JOHN HENEBRY
3RD ATTACK GROUP USAAF
DISTINGUISHED SERVICE CROSS, SILVER STAR,
4 DFCs, 2 AIR MEDALS, PURPLE HEART

I first flew the B-25 on submarine patrol on the East Coast. I converted to the A-20 in the Southwest Pacific. The A-20 was a twin-engine single-pilot airplane. I preferred the A-20 over the B-25 cockpit. Although it was designed for one pilot, it had the same engines as the B-25. Everything in the cockpit was very handy and laid out just right. The A-20 cockpit was a little better organized than the B-25, but just as noisy. It was very comfortable during long trips and the visibility was excellent. The A-20 was a little faster than the B-25 — about 20 miles per hour (42 km/h) faster — but it carried a smaller bomb load.

EXCERPT FROM A SECRET AIR FIGHTING DEVELOPMENT UNIT REPORT
RAF STATION DUXFORD. MARCH 16, 1941

INTERIM REPORT ON TACTICAL TRIALS OF DOUGLAS 'BOSTON' CLOSE SUPPORT BOMBER

Pilot's Cockpit: The cockpit is well laid out, placed in front of the air screws and affording the pilot an excellent all-round field of view, but the lack of a clear vision panel is a great disadvantage in rain and haze. The hood is 8 feet long (2.4 m) and hinged on the starboard side, giving easy access to the cockpit, but it is not robust, and closing it securely needs great care. Owing to its tendency to fly open in the air, a security clip was embodied by this unit which has proved satisfactory.

Conclusions: As a direct-support bomber, the Boston is an excellent aeroplane, having high maximum speed, manoeuvrability, excellent fields of view, and being capable of medium dive bombing.

DOUGLAS A-20G HAVOC
USAF MUSEUM, DAYTON, OHIO

1. THROTTLE
2. PROPELLER SPEED CONTROLS
3. MIXTURE CONTROLS
4. IGNITION SWITCHES
5. OUTSIDE AIR TEMP GAUGE
6. AIRSPEED INDICATOR
7. ARTIFICIAL HORIZON
8. CONTROL WHEEL
9. VSI

10. ADF
11. GUN BUTTON
12. COMPASS
13. TURN AND BANK INDICATOR
14. MAGNETO SWITCH
15. OIL PRESSURE GAUGE
16. FUEL PRESSURE GAUGE
17. CYLINDER HEAD TEMP GAUGE

18. OIL TEMP GAUGE
19. CARBURETTOR AIR TEMP
20. FUEL TANK SELECTOR
21. RADIO CONTROL BOX
22. CABIN HEAT CONTROL
23. BOMB SELECTOR
24. ELECTRICAL SWITCHES
25. PILOT'S SEAT
26. RUDDER PEDALS
27. DIRECTIONAL GYRO

A-20C ATTACK BOMBER WARMING UP.

FLYING FORTRESS

"Against the Luftwaffe, the capital enemy,
the rugged and steady B-17 remained the natural pick."
— Martin Caidin, *Flying Forts*

Many consider the B-17 to be the most famous American bomber of the Second World War. When first conceived, it was considered a defensive weapon and not the strategic bomber it would later become. In 1934, when the USAAC issued a requirement for a new multi-engine bomber, Boeing took the term "multi-engine" to mean more than two, which was the norm at the time. Work began on Model 299 in June 1934, and the prototype first flew on July 28, 1935. A local newspaper reporter nicknamed the new four-engine bomber "Flying Fortress," and the name stuck.

The first B-17Bs entered service in 1939, and at the time they were the fastest and the highest-flying bombers in the world. The U.S. Army Air Corps was also developing its long-range strategic bombing program. Using massed formations of B-17s, they believed the combined firepower of a large formation of aircraft would make interception by enemy fighters hazardous and ineffective. As the "phoney war" dragged on in Europe, Boeing continued to improve the B-17. Combat survivability was key. More armour, self-sealing tanks, and heavier defensive armament were added. The new B-17C was armed with the heavier hitting 0.50-inch machine guns in all positions except the nose. Only 38 B-17Cs were built: 18 for the USAAC and 20 for the Royal Air Force. Designated "Fortress I" in the RAF, the B-17C began operations with 90 Squadron.

Combat experience with the RAF revealed the B-17C was not ready for combat missions over Europe. The defensive armament was inadequate, guns froze at high altitude, and the Nordon bombsight did not live up to expectations. From these lessons, Boeing developed the B-17E, the first truly combat-ready model. The B-17E sported a giant dorsal fin and long-span tailplane, which improved high-altitude control. The armament was completely revised: a power turret was added behind the cockpit, a ventral turret at the trailing edge, and a new manual turret in the tail. Armament now consisted of ten 0.50-inch machine guns and two 0.30-inch machine guns.

In April 1942, B-17Es began flying combat missions with the 5th Air Force in Australia and the 7th Air Force in the Philippines. May 1942 saw the 92nd, 97th, and 301st Bomb Groups cross the Atlantic. On August 17, 1942, 18 B-17s from the 97th Bomb Group bombed rail marshalling yards in Northern France, signalling the beginning of the USAAF's daylight bombing campaign against Germany. The B-17E was soon rendered obsolete. The new F model appeared with over 400 modifications. Its range was extended, and new paddle-bladed propellers were added. Over 3,045 F models were produced. German fighter pilots soon learned to attack the B-17 head-on, as the nose-mounted guns proved ineffective. On August 17, 1943, the 8th Air Force sent 376 B-17s deep into Germany for the first time. Losses were appalling, with 60 Forts shot down, 100 damaged, and 35 damaged beyond repair.

In early 1944, the B-17G, with the new chin turret, entered service. With the introduction of the long-range P-51 Mustang, massive formations of B-17s could reach deep into Germany with great success. The last combat mission flown by the B-17 occurred on April 25, 1945. At the end of the Second World War, the B-17 equipped 106 squadrons (2,300 aircraft) in the U.K. and 24 squadrons (500 aircraft) in Italy.

Above: Factory fresh B-17G. In 1944 the all-metal finish replaced the standard olive drab.
Right: Test flight of a B-17G. *Inset*: First Lieutenant Albert Keeler, co-pilot on the 412th Bomb Squadron's "Full House."

THE PILOT'S
P E R S P E C T I V E
AIR VICE-MARSHAL
RON DICK
RAF (RET.), CB, FRAeS

Air Marshal Ron Dick became familiar with the cockpit of a very special B-17 in October 1993—a restored B-17G destined for the collection of the Royal Air Force Museum, at Hendon. He had never flown an aircraft with four piston engines before, but had nevertheless managed to talk his way into being the pilot to fly it from California to the U.K.

The cockpit of a B-17 is a pleasant place to work, but accessing it is another matter. Honour demands that pilots enter through the forward hatch, which is only some two feet square and six feet off the ground. The Gregory Peck entry involves grasping the outer edge of the hole with both hands, lifting and swinging both legs together through the opening, and then twisting them down the fuselage in the process, so that with a final heave and squirm the body is deposited on the cabin floor, quivering from exertion.

Once settled in the simple bucket seat, the pilot finds a more rational environment. Broadly speaking, the main instrument panel is divided into three, with the basic flying instruments set over the electric and hydraulic systems switches on the left, the radio equipment in the middle, and the engine instruments in front of the co-pilot.

The throttles tower out of their quadrant like a fireman's ladder. Grasp the top rung and engines one and four will respond, while the bottom rung gives you two and three. The split middle rung gives all four at once and is therefore used the most.

Viewed as a whole, the B-17 has a functional but welcoming cockpit. There is nothing plush or fancy about it, but all seems purposeful, and there is a lot of light. Indeed, the generous provision of transparent surface lends the aircraft a conservatory air. Delightful though that is for peacetime flying, it must have engendered a feeling of nakedness when the sky ahead was full of Luftwaffe fighters.

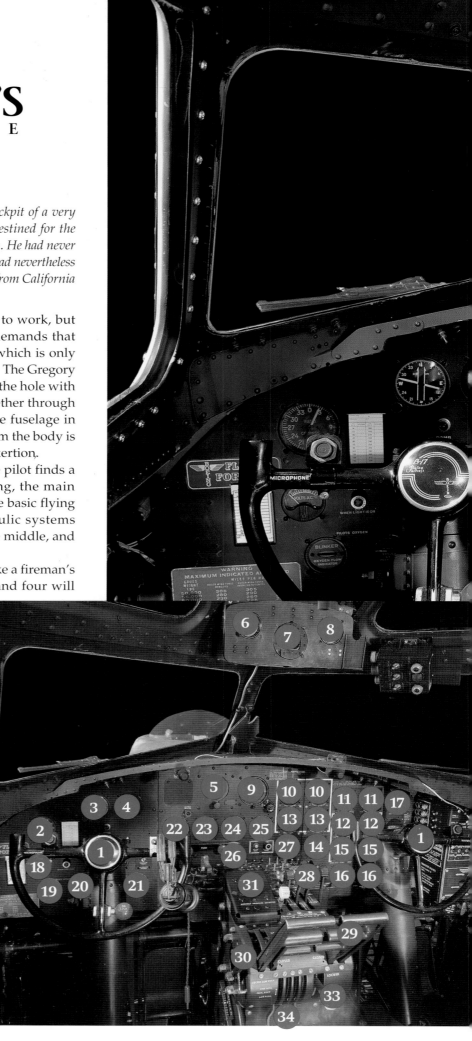

BOEING B-17G FORTRESS
USAF Museum, Dayton, Ohio

1. Control column
2. Radio compass
3. Remote compass indicator
4. Pilot's directional indicator
5. Turn indicator
6. Clock
7. Compass
8. De-icer pressure gauge
9. Artificial horizon
10. Manifold pressure gauges
11. Fuel pressure gauges
12. Oil pressure gauges
13. Tachometers
14. Flap position indicator
15. Oil temp gauges
16. Cylinder-head temp gauge
17. Free air temp gauge
18. Voltmeter
19-20. Pilot's oxygen flow indicator/ pressure
21. Co-pilot's oxygen flow indicator/ pressure
22. Altimeter
23. ASI
24. Turn and bank indicator
25. Rate of climb indicator
26. Propeller feathering switches
27. Bulb test button (far left), bomber call light (left), landing gear warning light (centre) , tailwheel lock light (right)
28. Mixture controls
29. Throttles
30. Throttle control lock
31. Turbo supercharger control
32. Intercooler controls
33. Propeller lock control
34. Propeller controls

CONSOLIDATED B-24
LIBERATOR

SOMEWHAT OVERSHADOWED BY THE FAMOUS BOEING B-17
FLYING FORTRESS, THE B-24 LIBERATOR EXPLOITS WERE MANY.
THE B-24 WAS TRULY UNIQUE IN AVIATION HISTORY.

Built in greater numbers than the B-17, the B-24 was produced in greater quantities than any other American aircraft. The first prototype did not fly until after the beginning of the Second World War, and when production finally came to an end, the number built totalled 18,188 (compared to 12,731 for the B-17 and 7,366 for the Lancaster). Even more remarkable was the B-24's operational record. B-24 Liberators operated over more operational fronts for longer periods of time and they were produced in a greater variety of variants than any other Allied aircraft.

When compared to the B-17 in the looks department, the Liberator could never compete. Although her crews may have loved her, the deep, slab-sided fuselage and huge vertical tail surfaces made the B-24 look slow and heavy. But appearances can be deceiving, for the B-24 would turn out to be one of the war's most versatile aircraft. Its first role was that of strategic bomber, but early on the Liberator was used for maritime and long-range reconnaissance, anti-submarine operations, passenger and transport, and as a flying tanker. It was even used as the personal transport for Winston Churchill. Because of its great range, the B-24 closed the gap in the Northwest Atlantic and turned the tide in the U-boat war.

The Liberator's great range would serve it well. B-24s were able to attack targets that were unreachable by other Allied aircraft. As a bomber, the B-24 was supreme; it could fly farther with a heavier bomb-load than the B-17, and it was also an effective fighter (credited with 2,600 enemy aircraft). It was the Allies' leading oceanic patrol aircraft and the leading long-range transport.

The Liberator was one of the most complicated and advanced machines in the Allied inventory. This complexity demanded prolonged pilot training. Compared to other four-engine bombers, the B-24 was demanding and unforgiving. Above 20,000 feet (6,096 m), the B-24 became too unstable to fly in close formation. Escape from a damaged machine was also extremely difficult once the pilot released the controls.

In 1942–43, the B-24D was in service in every theatre and was the most important long-range bomber in the Pacific. In the North Atlantic, 15 anti-submarine squadrons were employed. In the RAF, no fewer than 37 squadrons served in Coastal, Bomber, and Far East Commands. In their most famous action of the War, B-24Ds completed the long-range, low-level attacks on the Ploesti oil fields in Romania (one third of Germany's petroleum came from Ploesti). From their North African bases, B-24 crews practised ultra-low-level flying. It was assumed that the enemy would expect the bombers to come in at high altitude and that the low-level approach would achieve an element of surprise and thus create more damage. At the completion of the zero-altitude training, the mission was laid on. Codenamed "Tidal Wave," the attacking force consisted of 178 aircraft, of which 164 made it to target. Losses totalled 41 aircraft destroyed, 30 severely damaged, and 540 men killed.

One of the shortcomings with the B-24D was its vulnerability to head-on attack. The three handheld 0.50-inch machine guns in the nose proved inadequate, and despite modifications, the internal protection remained poor. In both Europe and the Pacific, pilots and waist gunners were being killed by shells that entered through the nose. Modifications soon followed, and the B-24G entered squadron service with a twin gun turret in the nose.

RIGHT: MAJOR BURNETT AND SGT. BENKO POSE FOR THE CAMERA IN THEIR B-24, CHINA.
ABOVE: CONSOLIDATED PB4Y-1, THE MARITIME PATROL VERSION OF THE B-24, FLYING OVER THE ENGLISH COUNTRY SIDE.

THE PILOT'S
PERSPECTIVE
COLONEL
H. BEN WALSH
USAF (RET.)

I was a Flight Commander in one of the three B-24 groups assigned to England in early 1943, and I flew until the end of the War. We flew the B-24D model, which I considered to be a stable aircraft. I had flown with a B-17 Group in 1942, and when I first got into the cockpit of the B-24 I was surprised by the tight fit. To climb into the cockpit decked out in a cumbersome sheepskin flying suit, flying boots, flak helmet, Mae West, and parachute, was no easy endeavour. For a tall guy such as myself, I found it to be a bit cramped. Once you were strapped into the cockpit you knew you were going to be there for a while. In my case, when I was shot down, I learned very quickly just how tight that cockpit was. It was not an easy airplane to exit in case of an emergency.

Once you were established in the cockpit, everything was well laid out. The throttles were located between you and the co-pilot, so either one of you could handle them. The supercharger was over on the pilot's side. I found the rpm gauge and throttles to be in a good position. The auto-pilot was in a good position also, over to the left of the throttle quadrant. That equipment came in very handy, because it could get you out of trouble if you had any severed cables.

I liked the B-24 cockpit. The flying instruments were well situated—all of them were directly in front of you. You had the trims tabs right beside the throttle quadrant, and you could literally lift the aircraft off with the trim tabs if you wanted to. In later models, the trim tab was vital because of the very heavy nose turret. I flew everything from the D to the J model. I found the D to be the most stable platform for close-formation flying.

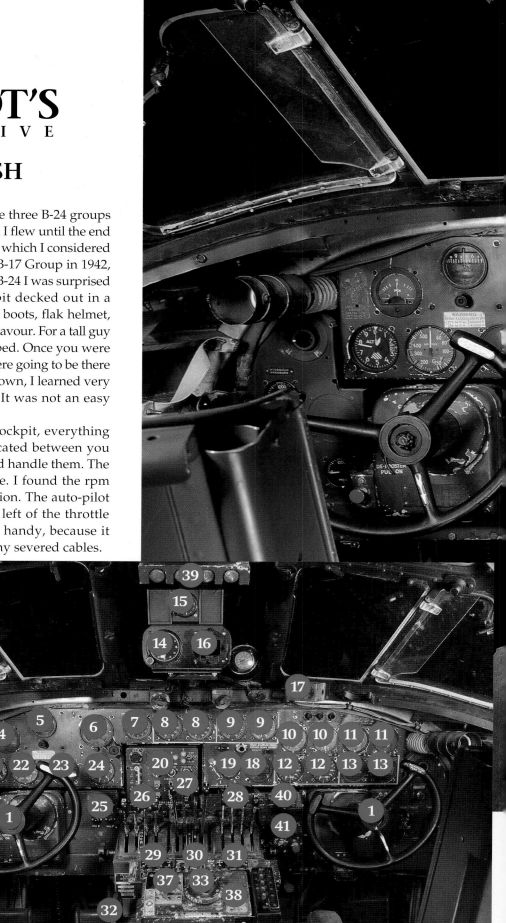

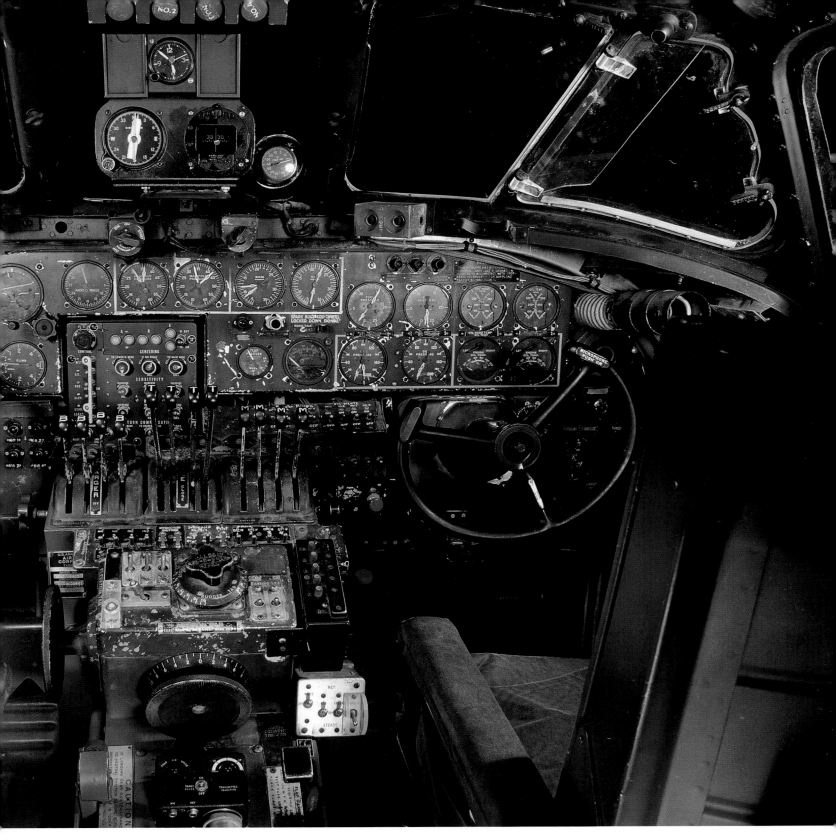

CONSOLIDATED B-24D LIBERATOR
USAF Museum, Dayton, Ohio

1. Control wheel
2. Defrosting tubes
3. Ventilator control
4. PDI
5. Turn indicator
6. Artificial horizon
7. Radio compass
8. Manifold pressure gauges
9. Tachometer
10. Fuel pressure gauges
11. Cylinder head temp gauges
12. Oil pressure gauges
13. Oil temp gauges
14. Automatic direction finder
15. Clock
16. Compass
17. Destruction switches
18. Free air temp gauge
19. Flap position gauge
20. AFC control box
21. Altimeter
22. ASI
23. Turn and bank indicator
24. Rate of climb indicator
25. Indicator lights
26. Supercharger controls
27. Throttles
28. Mixture controls
29. Recognition light switch box
30. Intercooler switches
31. Cowl flap switches
32. Elevator tab knob
33. Rudder tab knob
34. Aileron tab knob
35. Radio control
36. Landing gear handle
37. AC switches, passing light switch, alarm bell, horn interruption switch
38. Landing light switches
39. Propeller feathering push buttons
40. Booster pump switches, primer switches
41. Starter switches, oil dilution switches

NORTH AMERICAN B-25
MITCHELL

POTENT AND VERSATILE, THE B-25 MITCHELL WAS ARGUABLY THE BEST ALL-ROUND MEDIUM BOMBER OF THE SECOND WORLD WAR.

In the early twenties, air power was in its infancy. A far-sighted colonel by the name of William "Billy" Mitchell was court-marshalled for his outspoken views on the use of this new power. Named after the forthright colonel, the B-25 Mitchell would play an important role during the Second World War and in the end would help vindicate the prophetic colonel.

Designed in 1938, the B-25 first entered service in the spring of 1941 with the 17th Bombardment Group. After the attack on Pearl Harbor, the group was moved to the West Coast for coastal anti-submarine patrols. Success soon followed, as a Japanese submarine was sunk on December 24.

In the first six months of 1942, the Japanese seemed invincible. The Allies were continually on the defensive, with little hope for a decisive victory. But in April the B-25 Mitchell would participate in one of the War's most daring exploits. Sixteen aircraft from the 17th Bomb Group were modified to carry 1,141 gallons (4,319 litres) of fuel. The ventral turrets and Norden bombsights were removed, and wooden guns were fitted in the tail. Lieutenant Colonel James H. Doolittle called for volunteer pilots, and the 16 B-25Bs were loaded aboard the aircraft carrier USS *Hornet*. On April 18, 200 miles from the launch position the Task Force comprising the carriers *Hornet* and *Enterprise* was sighted by a Japanese patrol boat. 800 miles (1,287 km) from Japan and with only 467 feet (142 m) of carrier runway, the B-25s took off. Doolittle led his planes in low-level attacks on several Japanese cities. None of the aircraft

reached their prearranged airfields in China. Many crashed or force-landed, with the majority of crews escaping capture with the help of the Chinese. In the United States morale soared, while in Japan the humiliation was complete.

Regarded as one of the best aircraft in its class, the docile B-25 had excellent all-round performance. During the War, the Mitchell was used in almost every role appropriate to its size: high- and low-level bombing, strafing, photo reconnaissance, and anti-submarine patrol.

In the Pacific, it excelled as a low-level anti-shipping aircraft, and when heavier armament was called for, the B-25H appeared, with a lightweight 75-mm field gun in the nose. Armed with eight additional 0.50-inch guns firing forward, and two in each of the dorsal, waist, and tail positions, the B-25H was one of the most heavily armed aircraft to operate in the Pacific.

Used by the RAF, the Soviet Air Force, and other friendly air forces, the B-25 Mitchell was produced in greater numbers than any other American twin-engine bomber. In the RAF, over 800 B-25Cs, Ds, and Js served in Europe, and over 800 were shipped to the Soviet Union.

A total of 11,000 Mitchells were produced between 1940 and 1945, serving on every major front from North Africa to Burma. It was regarded as the best medium bomber of the War.

ABOVE: A B-25 HEADS OUT ON A TRAINING MISSION FROM THE AAF TACTICAL TRAINING CENTER AT ORLANDO, FLORIDA.
LEFT: AN ALL-BLACK NIGHT RECONNAISSANCE B-25 FROM THE 7TH PHOTO GROUP.
IT WAS THE ONLY B-25 TO SERVE WITH BOTH THE 8TH AND 9TH AIR FORCE.

THE PILOT'S
PERSPECTIVE
BROCK MASON
THE CANADIAN WARPLANE
HERITAGE MUSEUM

I have been flying the B-25 for the Canadian Warplane Heritage Museum for 12 years. My dad flew with RAF Ferry Command. He did a couple of trips in Mitchells, so when I first sat in the cockpit of the B-25 it was a real thrill. My first impression inside the cockpit of the B-25 was that it smelled like a real airplane. The cockpit is easy to get into. Some people think it's cramped, but once you're settled in there is ample room and it's really quite comfortable.

The instrument panel is not well laid out by modern standards. The instruments tend to be all over the place, with the exception of the centre stack, where you find the power, pressure, and fuel instruments. It is a vintage layout, but like all cockpits you get used to it. The power quadrant is very convenient and easy to use. All the switches— priming, starting, mags, masters — are all right there on the power quadrant and within easy reach.

The Americans flew the B-25 with a co-pilot, but the British flew with a single pilot. In the early part of the war, the British did not have the manpower to fill two seats. It was a lot for one pilot, but it could be done. By today's standards, the B-25 is definitely a two-pilot airplane.

The view through the canopy is good, but with the two big engines right there, your view is somewhat restricted. The B-25 is a docile and agile airplane for its vintage. The only critical characteristic of the aircraft is engine failure on take-off with a heavy load; it is a handful on one engine.

I like the B-25 cockpit. The visibility is certainly better than in the DC-3. It's also more comfortable, and with its tricycle landing gear, the visibility on the ground is very good. It's a great privilege to fly this airplane; it's also great fun.

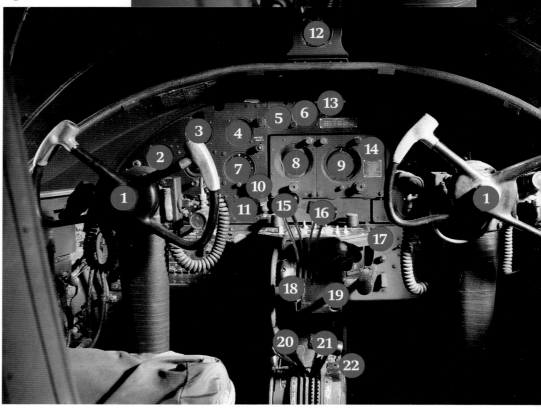

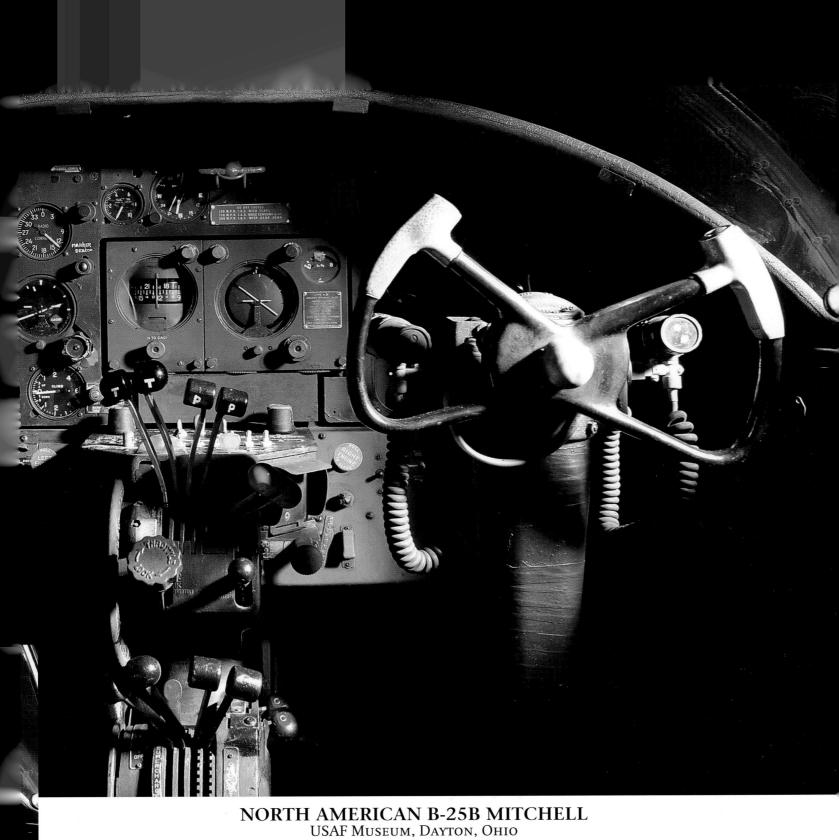

NORTH AMERICAN B-25B MITCHELL
USAF Museum, Dayton, Ohio

1. Control wheel
2. Airspeed indicator
3. ILS indicator
4. Radio compass
5. Suction gauge
6. Remote compass indicator
7. Gyro horizon
8. Turn indicator
9. Auto pilot-bank-climb gyro control unit
10. Artificial horizon lock control
11. Rate of climb indicator
12. Compass
13. Emergency bomb release handle
14. Auto pilot-vacuum gauge
15. Throttle controls
16. Propeller controls
17. Mixture controls
18. Throttle controls friction lock
19. Propeller controls friction lock
20. Supercharger controls
21. Oil cooler shutter controls
22. Carb air control

MARTIN B-26
MARAUDER

KNOWN EARLY ON AS THE "WIDOW MAKER," THE B-26 MARAUDER WOULD ESTABLISH THE LOWEST OPERATIONAL LOSS RATE OF ANY AMERICAN AIRCRAFT IN EUROPE.

In January 1939, the USAAC issued a requirement for a new, high-speed, long-range medium bomber capable of carrying a 2,000-pound (907 kg) bomb load. The worsening international situation called for expedience and, as such, no prototype was asked for. This became commonplace as the War progressed. Construction of the first B-26 took about one year. The first flight took place on November 25, 1940. When first introduced into the USAAF, the press dubbed it the "Flying Torpedo" because of its streamlined circular fuselage. But in service the Marauder soon earned the nickname "Widow Maker."

Because the design requirements did not specify landing and take-off speeds, the Marauder was able to obtain its impressive performance with a small wing area and high wing loading. Its landing speed of 130 miles per hour (209 km/h) and high wing loading resulted in many fatalities. As a consequence, four investigative boards convened to decide the Marauder's fate. Modifications were ordered and the wing and vertical tail were extended.

Immediately after Pearl Harbor, the 22nd Bomb Group moved to Australia. With extra fuel tanks in the bomb bay, these aircraft flew strikes against Japanese targets in New Guinea, and during the epic battle of Midway, torpedo-carrying Marauders made a small contribution. In the first 11 months of the War, B-26 operations were confined to the Pacific, but it was in Europe and the Mediterranean that the Marauder made its mark. Following the "Torch" landings in North Africa, the 17th, 319th, and 320th Bomb Groups, with the 12th Air Force, operated the B-26. In Northern Europe,

early Marauder operations were very disappointing. In the low-level attack role, the B-26 proved to be extremely vulnerable. On May 14, 1943, 10 Marauders bombed the Velsen generating station at Ijmuiden, in the Netherlands. The entire formation was destroyed by a combination of flak, fighters, and collision. In response, B-26 operations were moved to medium and high altitudes. It was not until the Marauder was assigned to the 9th Tactical Air Force that its full potential was realized. By May 1944, in preparation for the D-Day landings, the 9th Air Force had eight bomb groups, comprising 28 squadrons, ready for operations.

In the Royal Air Force, the B-26 first entered service in 1942. In the rapidly expanding South African Air Force, the Marauder was issued to five squadrons. The Free French also flew the B-26; by 1944 it equipped six squadrons. Under the Lend-Lease program, 525 Marauders were acquired by the RAF.

In total, 5,157 examples of the Marauder were produced. It left its mark in every theatre of war in which it fought. Despite its early problems, the later versions of the Marauder had no particularly vicious flying characteristics. But because of its advanced design, it did demand a high level of pilot training. In return though, the Marauder offered a certain level of operational immunity. The Marauder's war record was impressive: 129,943 operational sorties flown in Europe and the Mediterranean; 169,382 tons (153,663 tonnes) of bombs dropped; 402 enemy aircraft destroyed—all for a loss of just 911 aircraft in combat. This data represented a loss rate of less than one percent—the lowest loss rate of any American aircraft in the European theatre.

BELOW: 8TH AIR FORCE B-26 MARAUDERS LINE UP FOR TAKE-OFF.
RIGHT: B-26 MARAUDERS HAVE JUST UNLOADED THEIR BOMBS ON A ROAD AND RAIL JUNCTION IN FRANCE.

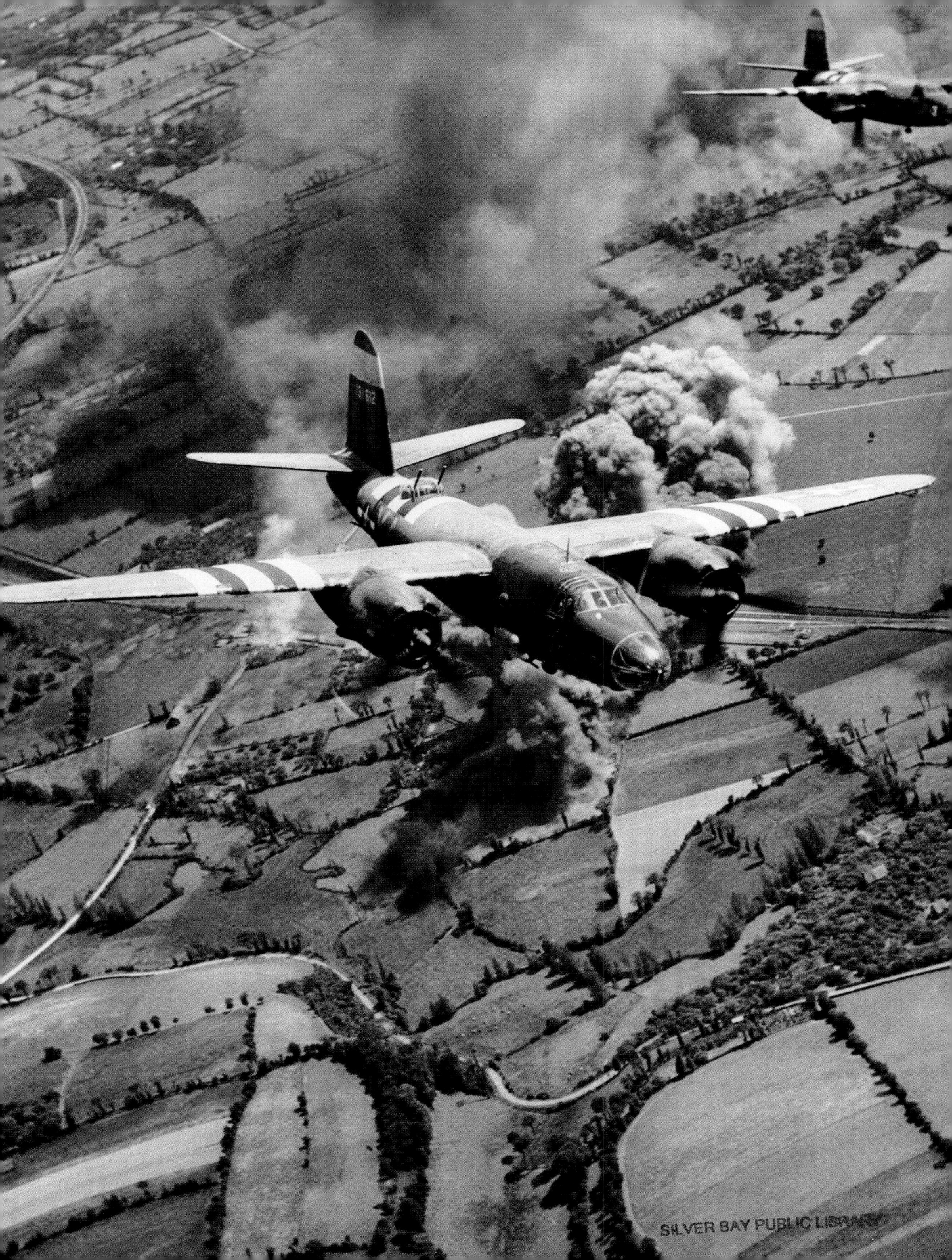

THE PILOT'S
P E R S P E C T I V E
LIEUTENANT COLONEL
JACK K. HAVENER
USAF (RET.), PURPLE HEART, DFC
EUROPEAN CAMPAIGN MEDAL WITH FIVE STARS

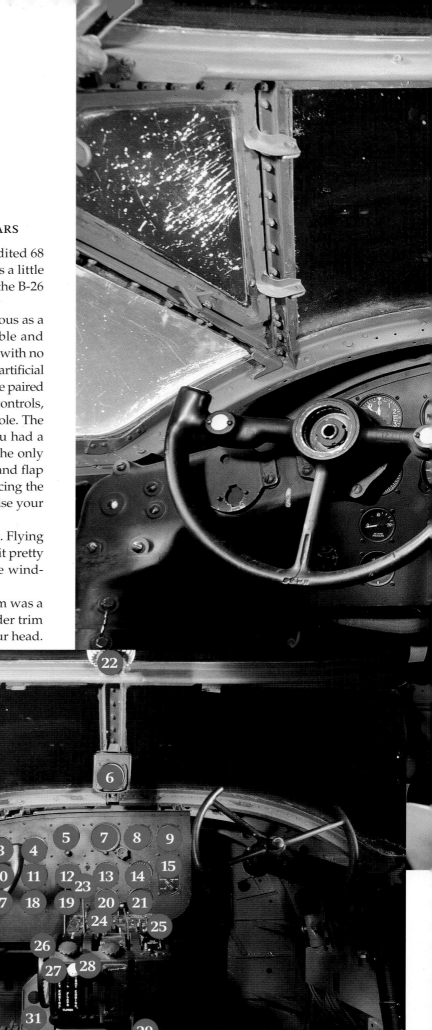

I went over to Europe in January 1944 and was credited 68 missions. When I first sat in the B-26 cockpit it was a little overwhelming. Coming off twin-engine trainers, the B-26 was a bit of a shock, but that soon wore off.

The cockpit was easy to get into. It wasn't as spacious as a Stratocruiser, but the pilot's seat was very comfortable and shielded with armour plating. The cockpit was spartan, with no luxuries, but the instrument panel was well laid out. The artificial horizon was centre top, and your engine instruments were paired up. I thought it was a good layout. The throttles, prop controls, and mixture controls were all handy on the centre console. The switches for the propellers were also right there. If you had a runaway propeller, you just hit the decrease switch. The only thing I didn't like was the location of the landing gear and flap levers. They were located on the back of the console, facing the rear of the aircraft. If you weren't careful you would raise your gear instead of your flaps!

Heating in the B-26 cockpit was always a problem. Flying at 12,000 feet (6,658 m) over Europe in the winter made it pretty cold. The heat that we did have was used to keep the windscreen clear.

The B-26 was a trim-tab airplane. The elevator trim was a wheel on the left-hand side of the console and the rudder trim control was a crank that was located up and behind your head. That could be a little hairy. You had to trim the B-26 constantly, but once you got it trimmed it would really go. The B-26 was an excellent formation flier. That's why the German fighters didn't bother us much.

The B-26 was a pleasure to fly. It could take a hell of a lot of punishment and still get you home. I thought it was great.

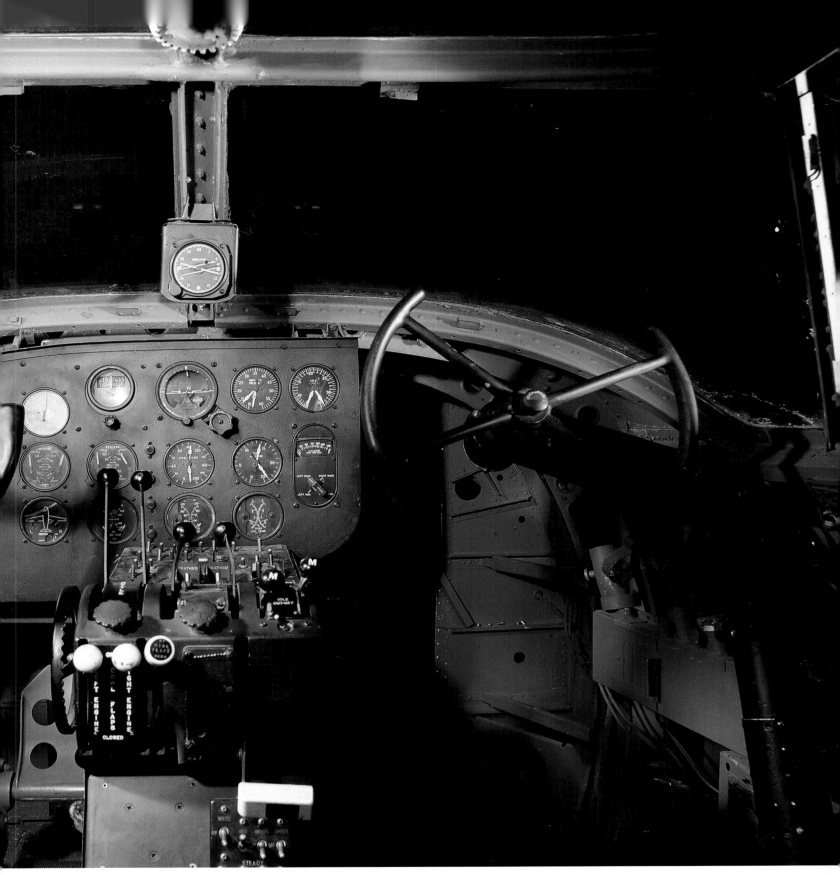

MARTIN B-26G MARAUDER
USAF MUSEUM, DAYTON, OHIO

1. CONTROL WHEEL
2. ALTIMETER
3. TURN AND BANK
4. AIRSPEED INDICATOR
5. DIRECTIONAL GYRO
6. MAGNESYN COMPASS
7. ARTIFICIAL HORIZON
8. MANIFOLD PRESSURE GAUGE

9. TACHOMETER INDICATOR
10. VSI
11. OIL TEMP GAUGE
12. OIL TEMP GAUGE
13. OIL PRESSURE GAUGE
14. FUEL PRESSURE GAUGE
15. FUEL QUANTITY GAUGE AND SELECTOR
16. FREE AIR THERMOMETER

17. SUCTION GAUGE
18. COWL FLAPS AND OIL COOLER FLAPS POSITION INDICATOR
19. LANDING GEAR AND WING FLAPS POSITION INDICATOR
20. CARBURETTOR AIR TEMP GAUGE
21. CYLINDER HEAD TEMP GAUGE
22. RUDDER TRIM TAB CONTROL
23. THROTTLES

24. PROPELLER GOVERNOR CONTROLS
25. MIXTURE CONTROLS
26. ELEVATOR TRIM TAB CONTROL
27. COWL FLAP CONTROLS
28. WING FLAPS CONTROL
29. LANDING GEAR CONTROL
30. RECOGNITION LIGHT SWITCHES
31. RUDDER PEDALS

BOEING B-29
SUPERFORTRESS

STARTED THREE YEARS BEFORE THE SECOND WORLD WAR BEGAN,
THE B-29 WOULD BECOME THE WORLD'S FIRST FULLY PRESSURIZED BOMBER.
IN THE END, IT WOULD ALSO BE THE MOST FAMOUS.

In the late 1930s, the U.S. military began to consider the possibility of an Axis invasion of the Americas. The concept of hemisphere defence called for a bomber capable of long range and a sizeable bomb load. This was the starting point for the aircraft that was to become the world's first atomic bomber.

In 1938, the Boeing Aircraft Company began looking at plans to produce an improved B-17 with a pressurized cabin. This study, along with many others, led to the Boeing Model 345, which featured a high-aspect wing, engine nacelles designed to minimize drag, and a tricycle undercarriage. In 1940, the new bomber, designated the B-29, was ready for production. The U.S. Army Air Corps ordered two prototypes.

The Wright 2,200-horsepower R-3350 engine was chosen for the B-29. At the time, it was the most powerful engine to be installed in an aircraft. Boeing was confident the new bomber could reach 30,000 feet (9,145 m), but many problems lay ahead. After the attack on Pearl Harbor, a colossal manufacturing program was implemented. The Wichita plant was expanded and a new factory at Renton was built for B-29 production. Work on the aircraft became a priority, and new production lines were soon started in Georgia and Omaha. In all, over 60 new factories began making components—all before the first B-29 had even flown.

The XB-29 prototype first flew on September 21, 1942, and the second on December 28, 1942. The B-29 was a technical marvel; no other aircraft even came

BELOW: TWO YB-29S IN FLIGHT. *ABOVE RIGHT:* B-29S UNLOAD THEIR LETHAL CARGO.

close to its level of sophistication. The aircraft was divided into three pressurized sections. The cockpit area contained the pilot, navigator, bombardier, flight engineer, and radio operator. The centre section, connected to the cockpit by a tunnel over the bomb bay, held the gunner's station and rest area. Finally, the tail gunner had his own separate pressurized compartment. The flight-testing program was plagued by engine failures and fires, and in February 1943, the second XB-29 crashed. As testing continued, it became clear that the B-29 was a winner, but the technical snags were many and they had multiplied. As the first B-29s came off the production lines, they were immediately sent to the modification centre at Salina, Kansas. There, 600 men modified and repaired over 9,900 faults in the first 175 aircraft.

On June 5, 1944, the first B-29 bombing mission was flown, from Kharagpur, India. Eighty aircraft flew the 2,000-mile (3,219 km) round trip and bombed railway targets in Bangkok. Results were poor, as only 18 bombs landed on target. On June 15, Japan was raided for the first time. From this point on, the buildup of Superfortess bases was slow and scattered. It was not until the capture of the Mariana Islands of Saipan, Guam, and Tinian that the B-29 bombing campaign began in earnest. Early results were not encouraging. The high-altitude bombing tactics were marred by jet-stream winds and small bomb loads.

In January 1945, Major General Curtiss E. LeMay was given command of the Marianas-based Super-fortresses. He changed the role of the B-29 from high-altitude daylight precision bomber, to low-level night bomber. On March 9, 1943, 334 Superfortresses created a fire storm in Tokyo. It was the most destructive bombing raid of the War! Sixteen square miles of Tokyo were burned out, and over 80,000 people lost their lives. In the following days, four more cities were attacked and over 32 square miles (83 km^2) were totally destroyed.

On August 6, 1945, the B-29 *Enola Gay* dropped the first atomic bomb on Hiroshima. Just three days later, on August 9, *Bock's Car* dropped the second on Nagasaki. Within five days, the War was over.

THE PILOT'S
P E R S P E C T I V E
BRIGADIER GENERAL
HENRY C. HUGLIN
USAF (RET.)

I first flew the B-29 during the 9th Bomb Group training in McCook, Nebraska. Our training started in June 1944 and ended in December when we deployed to Tinian in the Marianas. I flew the B-17 and B-24 as well, and when I first sat in the B-29 cockpit I was surprised by how much room there was. The wonderful glass nose was so much more open and the visibility was exceptional. The cockpit in the B-29 was very comfortable and well designed.

At that time, the B-29 was the most advanced aircraft in the world. The instrumentation was well laid out, the throttles were in a good position, and everything was functional and available. The B-29 was also the first bomber equipped with a pressurized cabin, which meant we didn't have to wear our oxygen masks at high altitude (they were always close by in case of decompression caused by battle damage, but that didn't happen very often). For a combat aircraft, the B-29 was remarkably restful. It was certainly less fatiguing than the B-17 and B-24. A typical bombing mission to Japan was 1,500 miles (2,414 km) there and back, which ran between 13 and 15 hours. Because the B-29 cockpit was so roomy, you could get up and stretch, which you really couldn't do in the B-17 or B-24.

The designed take-off weight for the B-29 was around 120,000 pounds (52,320 kg). We often pushed that up to around 137,000 pounds (62,143 kg) without any problems. Although we were based on the largest airfield in the world, with four 8,500-foot (2,591 m) runways, we often used every last inch to get airborne.

The B-29 was very advanced. It was also probably the most comfortable combat aircraft produced during the Second World War.

THE DECORATED NOSE OF "FLYING STUD II."

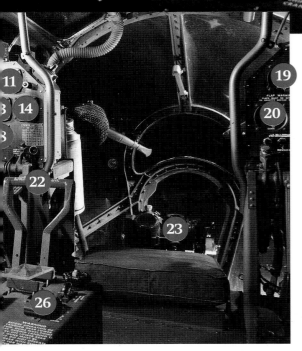

BOEING B-29 SUPERFORTRESS "BOCK'S CAR"
USAF Museum, Dayton, Ohio

1. Throttles
2. Control wheel
3. Airspeed indicator
4. Turn and bank indicator
5. Rate of climb indicator
6. Instrument for atomic bomb drop
7. Instrument for atomic bomb drop
8. Artificial horizon
9. Pilot direction indicator
10. Manifold pressure gauge
11. Manifold pressure gauge
12. Flux gate compass
13. Tachometer
14. Tachometer
15. Trim wheel
16. Ash tray
17. Turret warning lights
18. Radio compass
19. Altimeter
20. Flap position indicator
21. Rudder pedal
22. Emergency brakes
23. Norden bombsight
24. Flight control lock
25. Flap switch
26. Landing gear switch
27. Turbo supercharger boost control
28. Auto pilot controls
29. Pilot's seat

GRUMMAN F4F
WILDCAT

WHAT IT LACKED IN PURE FLYING PERFORMANCE, THE WILDCAT MORE THAN MADE UP FOR IN SUPERIOR ARMAMENT, RUGGED CONSTRUCTION, AND MOST IMPORTANTLY, AVAILABILITY.

During the crucial summer of 1942, it was the Wildcat that fought the numerically superior Japanese. Outclassed by the brilliant Zero, the Wildcat had to rely on its rugged construction and dive and zoom tactics to survive. The F6F Hellcat was a full year away, and the F4U Corsair would not arrive on Guadalcanal until early 1943. Production of the Wildcat in the first year of the war barely met attrition: 197 produced; 115 lost. Despite its performance deficiencies, the Wildcat still managed to amass an impressive combat record. In those crucial opening months of the war, it was the Wildcat that helped stop the Japanese and gave the Allies the time it so desperately needed to slowly build its forces.

First flown on September 2, 1937, the Wildcat was almost not built. A U.S. Navy requirement for a new carrier-based fighter went to the Brewster Aeronautical Corporation, who produced the woeful F2A-1 Buffalo. The F2A became the U.S. Navy's first operational monoplane fighter. The history of the Pacific War would have been very different if this airplane had been accepted for widespread service. The F2A Buffalo did not live up to its promise, and so the Navy authorized one prototype from Grumman.

The Wildcat's combat debut occurred on Christmas Day, 1940. A world away from the Pacific, a section of Wildcats (Martlets in the FAA) from 804 Squadron, Fleet Air Arm, intercepted a Ju 88 reconnaissance bomber over Scapa Flow. That same month, VF-4 accepted the U.S. Navy's first F4F Wildcat.

At the time of Pearl Harbor, the U.S. Navy and Marine Corps had 131 Wildcats in operational service. The Wildcat's first aerial victories in the Pacific came during the heroic defence of Wake Island. With a handful of Wildcats, the Marine pilots managed to shoot down eight enemy aircraft and sink two ships before being overwhelmed by the Japanese.

In air-to-air combat, the Mitsubishi Zero was clearly superior to the tubby Grumman Wildcat. The Zero was faster, had a better rate of climb, and could out-turn the Wildcat with ease. But in the early days of the war, in the desperate battles around Guadalcanal, the Coral Sea, Wake Island, and Midway, the Wildcat held its own. Using its superior diving characteristics, the Wildcat squadrons devised hit and run tactics. When Japanese aircraft were detected, the Wildcats would scramble and gain as much altitude as possible. With the height advantage, the Wildcats were able to dive on the enemy formations, aim for the bombers, and, before the escorting Zeros could intercept, climb back to altitude for another attack.

The combination of the Wildcat's superior armament and rugged construction with these hit and run tactics helped defeat the more nimble Zero and set the stage for Allied victories in the future.

On the other side of the world, Wildcats did valuable work providing convoy escort and anti-submarine patrols. It was the Wildcat that provided fighter cover during the Allied landings in North Africa, Madagascar, Italy, and Normandy. In the Battle of the Atlantic, the Wildcat contribution cannot be understated. Operating from MAC ships and escort carriers, Wildcats helped defeat the U-boat threat by shooting down Luftwaffe long-range reconnaissance aircraft and by teaming up with Swordfish aircraft to hunt submarines.

The Wildcat was the only U.S. Navy fighter to see continuous service from 1940 until the end of the war.

ABOVE: F4F-3S FROM THE FIGHTING SIX (VF-6) HAVE RED CROSSES APPLIED TO THE WINGS AND FUSELAGE FOR WAR GAMES IN 1941.
LEFT: FM-2 WILDCATS PRACTISE LANDINGS ON THE USS *CHARGER*.
INSET: F4F-4 WILDCATS READY FOR TAKE-OFF ABOARD A U.S. NAVY ESCORT CARRIER.

THE PILOT'S
P E R S P E C T I V E
FLIGHT LIEUTENANT
R.F. RON HITCHCOCK
RAF (RET.)

This aircraft—one of the earlier North American fighters—was used by the Fleet Air Arm (FAA) early in the War. The cockpit shows a certain amount of RAF and FAA thinking. That is, it's simple. If there is one characteristic criticism that I would give to the American cockpits in general, it's that they were overcomplicated. From my experience, you don't want that. You want things to be simple, and this cockpit is. It's well laid out, which means you can scan your instruments quickly without getting lost in a mass of instrumentation and switches.

There's plenty of room. I could feel very much at home in it. You've got very good visibility, but you also get the feeling that the front windscreen is rather a long way away. There's quite a distance from the front panel to the windscreen, but of course the gunsight would be there. I personally would like to have the front windscreen closer. It is a very nice cockpit, there's no doubt about that. Everything is at hand, which is good, as this aircraft doesn't have hydraulic landing gear. On this one you have to wind it up with your right arm. I don't think you would want to do that too often.

The Wildcat has a slightly different blind flying panel than what I am used to. On British aircraft of the period you have the rectangular blind flying panel. The visibility of this aircraft is not as good as, say, the Hellcat, but the thing that strikes me is how simple and straightforward the cockpit is. This is a big plus. I think Grumman got it right.

WILDCAT PILOT READY FOR TAKE-OFF.

GRUMMAN FM-2 WILDCAT
THE FIGHTER COLLECTION, DUXFORD, ENGLAND

1. PROPELLER SELECTION SWITCH
2. FUEL HANDPUMP
3. FUEL GAUGE
4. ALTIMETER
5. DIRECTIONAL GYRO
6. GUN SIGHT
7. ARTIFICIAL HORIZON
8. AIR SPEED INDICATOR
9. TURN AND BANK INDICATOR
10. RATE OF CLIMB INDICATOR
11. BOOST GAUGE
12. COMPASS
13. FUEL OIL PRESSURE GAUGE
14. ADF AUTOMATIC DIRECTION FINDER
15. RUDDER PEDAL
16. GENERATOR SWITCHES
17. UNDERCARRIAGE CONTROL
18. VOLT/AMMETER
19. CYLINDER PRIMING PUMP
20. UNDERCARRIAGE RATCHET RELEASE
21. UNDERCARRIAGE MECHANICAL INDICATOR
22. FUEL PUMP SWITCH

GRUMMAN F6F
HELLCAT

*"It was fast, well-armed, easy to fly. In short, the Hellcat was
a masterpiece of carrier-aircraft engineering and design."*
— Barret Tillman, *Hellcat Aces of World War II*

After the attack on Pearl Harbor and the subsequent battles in the Coral Sea and Guadalcanal, it became evident that a replacement for the Grumman F4F Wildcat was desperately needed. Work on the F6F began in June 1941. Initially, the F6F was to be an improved-version F4F, but reports from the Royal Navy and U.S. Navy called for a fighter with much higher performance. Before Pearl Harbor, Grumman had a design for a much larger and faster aircraft powered by the Pratt & Whitney R-2800 Double Wasp. In the following months, the F6F would emerge to become one of the truly great fighter aircraft of the Pacific War.

In less than a year, the first production model came off the assembly line. It was an amazing feat of design and manufacturing, and by the end of the War, over 10,000 Hellcats had been produced. Compared to the graceful lines and performance of the Spitfire, the F6F Hellcat was always the bridesmaid and never the bride. But when it came to the work it was designed for—carrier operations in the Pacific—the Hellcat had no peer.

Powered by a 2,000-horsepower Pratt & Whitney R-2800 Double Wasp engine, the Hellcat was faster, more manoeuvrable, more rugged, better armed, and could fly higher than the Mitsubishi Zero. U.S. Navy squadrons began to receive their new fighters on January 16, 1943, and from that point on, the Hellcat would accept the major responsibility for destroying the Japanese air forces. The Hellcats were well received in the fleet, and by August 1943, they were serving aboard the fleet carriers USS *Essex*, *Yorktown*, and *Independence*, and the light carriers USS *Belleau* and *Princetown*.

In the fighter's first big combat operation, 91 Hellcats attacked a force of 50 Zeros in the Kwajalein area. The Navy pilots destroyed 28 Zeros and lost only two Hellcats.

In order to protect the fleet from nocturnal raiders, the Hellcat was fitted with the 3-cm AN/APS-6 airborne radar. On November 26, 1943, using this radar, Lieutenant Commander "Butch" O'Hare disrupted a formation of Japanese bombers and saved the task force from attack. In one of the biggest air battles of the War, known as the "Marianas Turkey Shoot," Hellcats were able to shoot down over 400 enemy aircraft. This effectively wiped out the last remaining cadre of experienced Japanese pilots. From 1943 on, the Hellcat was the dominant fighter in almost all major air campaigns. It was flown by all of the U.S. Navy aces of that period. The Navy's leading ace was Commander David McCampbell, with a score of 34 Japanese aircraft shot down and 21 more destroyed on the ground. All of this was completed in just one tour of duty. Of the 6,477 Japanese aircraft U.S. Navy carrier pilots claimed to have destroyed in the air, the Hellcat was responsible for 4,947—an incredible feat considering the Hellcat did not enter combat service until August 31, 1943.

Well known for its exploits in the Pacific, the Hellcat also served in the Atlantic and Mediterranean with the British Fleet Air Arm. The FAA received 400 F6F Hellcats under the Lend-Lease Program. At first it was called the Grumman Gannet Mk I, but the name "Hellcat" was soon standardized. In operations off Norway, Hellcats provided top cover for the famous strikes against the German battleship *Tirpitz*.

The Hellcat's accident rate was lower than that of any other contemporary Navy aircraft—a vital statistic when one considers that more aircraft were lost in deck landing accidents than in enemy action.

Above: F6F-3 with gear down. F6Fs along with F4U Corsairs dominated the Pacific carrier war. *Right*: Hook down,
a Hellcat glides in for a landing aboard the USS *Randolph*. *Inset*: Hellcat about to take-off from USS *Charger*.

THE PILOT'S
P E R S P E C T I V E
STEPHEN GREY
THE FIGHTER COLLECTION

The F6F cockpit is a typical American cockpit. It's built for a big guy. There's plenty of room, maybe even too much room; you could find yourself rattling around in it. Aside from that, it is extremely comfortable, logical, simple, and straightforward.

It has a standard U.S. Navy-style control panel—very well laid out and easy to see. You've got the airspeed indicator (in knots), turn indicator, gyro rpm gauge, and manifold gauge. Down in the bottom right-hand corner are all your engine instruments—cylinder head temperature gauge, oil temperature, oil pressure, fuel pressure, and all the usual gizmos. The throttle controls are easy to hand and visibility is good. Being a carrier-borne aircraft, the Hellcat was designed with good low-speed handling in mind. Any old fool, including me, could fly it.

Below the panel are various emergency controls, such as emergency gear lowering and wing-fold safety control. On service airplanes they had a map table that you could pull out from underneath the control panel, which proved useful for long flights over the ocean. I think the reputation and the history of this airplane is an indication of how comfortable the pilots who flew it were. Some think the 11:1 kill ratio had to do with the fact that most of the good Japanese pilots had been killed earlier on and the remaining pilots weren't as well trained. I think it had a lot to do with the airplane.

In the F6F, you quickly feel at home. The ailerons are not great, but the rudder is fantastic, and it has a light wing loading. It's robust, simple, straightforward, and well armed. A very good fighter.

GRUMMAN
F6F-3 HELLCAT
THE FIGHTER
COLLECTION,
DUXFORD, ENGLAND

1. IGNITION SWITCH
2. CLOCK
3. ARTIFICIAL HORIZON
4. MAGNETIC COMPASS
5. DIRECTIONAL GYRO
6. TACHOMETER
7. SUCTION GAUGE
8. ACCELEROMETER
9. ALTIMETER
10. AIRSPEED INDICATOR
11. TURN AND BANK INDICATOR
12. RATE OF CLIMB INDICATOR
13. MANIFOLD PRESSURE GAUGE
14. LANDING GEAR EMERGENCY LOWER CONTROL
15. VOR
16. WING FOLD SAFETY LOCK
17. CYLINDER HEAD TEMP GAUGE
18. OIL PRESSURE GAUGE
19. OIL-IN TEMP GAUGE
20. FUEL QUANTITY GAUGE
21. FUEL PRESSURE GAUGE
22. CONTROL COLUMN
23. STARTER SWITCH
24. MANUAL RESET CIRCUIT BREAKER PANEL

NAVY ACE DAVID McCAMPBELL GIVES THE "THUMBS UP" AFTER ANOTHER SUCCESSFUL MISSION.

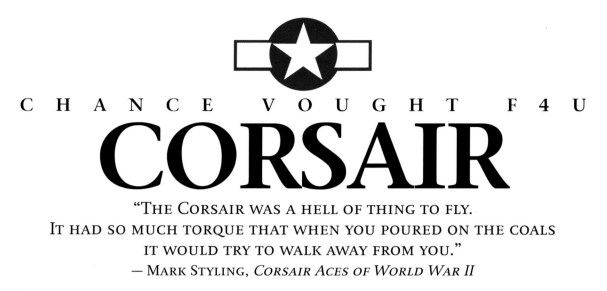

CHANCE VOUGHT F4U
CORSAIR

"THE CORSAIR WAS A HELL OF THING TO FLY.
IT HAD SO MUCH TORQUE THAT WHEN YOU POURED ON THE COALS
IT WOULD TRY TO WALK AWAY FROM YOU."
— MARK STYLING, *CORSAIR ACES OF WORLD WAR II*

The F4U Corsair was a truly remarkable aircraft and one of best piston-engine fighters to see service in the Second World War. It was also a killer. Responsible for an impressive number of enemy aircraft destroyed, in the hands of an inexperienced pilot, the Corsair was a handful to fly, and when something went wrong—pilot error or mechanical failure—the result was often fatal, resulting in the deaths of a large number of American and British pilots.

The Corsair was a technical masterpiece of advanced thinking and structural ingenuity. Designed in 1938, the first prototype did not emerge until two years later. Using the Pratt & Whitney R-2800 radial engine, the Corsair would have the largest propeller ever used on a single-seat fighter. To ensure proper ground clearance, the gull wing was incorporated, thus giving the Corsair its distinctive shape. The adaption of this wing also allowed for a relatively short undercarriage. The Corsair was a formidable aircraft with many innovative features: backward-retracting undercarriage, built-in long-range fuel tanks, and a hydraulic system to fold the wings and lower the deck hook.

The first prototype XF4U-1 took to the air on May 29, 1940, and the initial production order was issued on June 30. The first Corsairs to arrive in the

BELOW: SIX FAU-1 CORSAIRS OF VMF-222 AT VELLA LAVELLA ISLAND, DECEMBER 1943. NOTE THE SOLITARY WILDCAT IN BACKGROUND.

Pacific were flown by Marines. On February 12, 1943, 24 F4U-1s landed on Guadalcanal. With their superior range and endurance, the F4U could finally take the fight to the enemy. Long-range bomber escort was now possible, and fighter sweeps became the norm.

The F4U Corsair outperformed the Zero in every aspect but low-speed manoeuvrability and slow-speed rate of climb. Armed with six 0.50-inch machine guns with 400 rounds per gun, the Corsair's firepower was more than adequate. Most Japanese aircraft did not have armour plating or self-sealing tanks, and a two-second burst from the Corsair would fire 150 rounds of armour-piercing, tracer, and incendiary bullets. The result was almost always fatal.

Originally designed as a carrier-based fighter, the Navy deemed the Corsair unsuitable for carrier operations. Senior U.S. Navy aviators believed the F4U-1 was far too difficult for the average pilot to master and land on the deck of an aircraft carrier. As a result, U.S. Navy units were equipped with F6F Hellcats until the F4U was cleared for deck operations.

Unconcerned by the F4U's reputation, the British were the first to use the Corsair on carrier operations. From mid-1943, Corsair units trained for "blue water" ops, and in April 1944, they flew their first strikes against the German battleship *Tirpitz*. The U.S. Navy finally cleared the Corsair for deck operations in 1944.

By the end of the War, Corsairs were in service with the Marines, the US Navy, the Royal New Zealand Air Force, and the Fleet Air Arm. Over 2,140 Japanese aircraft were claimed destroyed, with a loss of only about 190 F4Us. Unfortunately, due to the Corsair's demanding flying characteristics, a greater number of Corsairs were lost to non-enemy action. In 1945, F4Us were pouring off the assembly line at the rate of 300 a month. They would stay in production until 1947. In fact, the F4U Corsair would enjoy the longest production run of any American piston-engine fighter.

When flown by well-trained, competent pilots, the F4U Corsair was a lethal opponent. Not only could it outfly the best Japanese fighters, it could outperform most Allied fighters as well.

Above: The bent-wing Corsair F4U-1 was the world's first naval aircraft to exceed 400 mph in level flight.

THE PILOT'S
PERSPECTIVE
STEPHEN GREY
THE FIGHTER COLLECTION

I don't know why they bent the wings on the Corsair. Everybody else managed to get a prop and engine of this size on straight wings. The theory is that it was done in order to clear the prop. But by doing that, they made everything more complicated, including getting onto the airplane and into the cockpit. It is also one of the more complex fighters in terms of cockpit layout. At the back of the left-hand side of the cockpit you have the controls to fold, unfold, and lock the wings. Close to those are the drop tank levers. You have a tail wheel lock, and, instead of the usual cluster that we see in other American fighters, you've got three separate gear boxes for the trim control.

One of the things you don't want to do in this aircraft is drop your map, because you'll never see it again. In later models, they put in a floor.

On the left-hand side, you have the fuel selector. The Corsair had two 150-gallon (568 l) dropable tanks, one on the right and one on the left. Together with internal fuel this airplane could go forever. The instrumentation is exactly the same as on other naval aircraft, with the basic navigation instruments at the top and the engine instruments down on the right-hand side.

It's a big cockpit, with lots of room. The first models had a birdcage canopy, but because you were behind the wing, the view ahead was not very good. In later models, they lifted the seat and canopy up so the pilot could see better. The cockpit was not ergonomically designed, but it remains fairly comfortable. Because you sit behind the wing, when you pull back on the stick, you go down as the nose goes up. It is a peculiar sensation that takes some getting used to.

CHANCE VOUGHT FG-1D CORSAIR
OLD FLYING MACHINE COMPANY, DUXFORD, ENGLAND

1. VACUUM GAUGE	9. ADS	18. FUEL OIL PRESSURE GAUGE
2. AIRSPEED INDICATOR	10. VOR	19. TACHOMETER
3. MAGNETIC COMPASS	11. ARTIFICIAL HORIZON	20. FLAP POSITION INDICATOR
4. FUEL GAUGE	12. VSI	21. IGNITION SWITCH
5. ALTIMETER	13. MANIFOLD PRESSURE GAUGE	22. AUXILIARY DROP TANK CONTROL
6. CARBURETTOR TEMP GAUGE	14. ACCELEROMETER	23. EXTINGUISHER BUTTON
7. INDICATOR LIGHT	15. TURN AND BANK INDICATOR	24. CONTROL COLUMN
8. CLOCK	16. VOR	25. UNDERCARRIAGE POSITION INDICATORS
	17. DIRECTIONAL GYRO	26. LANDING GEAR LEVER

FLEET AIR ARM F4U-1S AT
SQUANTUM, MASSACHUSETTS, 1943.

DAUNTLESS

CREWS CALLED IT THE "BARGE" OR THE "CLUNK,"
AND THOUGH IT WAS UNDERPOWERED AND PAINFULLY SLOW,
THE DAUNTLESS WAS THE MOST SUCCESSFUL SHIPBOARD DIVE BOMBER OF ALL TIME.

As the U.S. Navy's principal shipboard dive bomber, the Dauntless was the only U.S. aircraft to participate in all five carrier-versus-carrier engagements in the Pacific. Vulnerable, lacking in range, and exhausting to fly, the Dauntless still managed to emerge with an almost legendary reputation. This had more to do with the skill of its crews than with the aircraft itself.

First delivered to the U.S. Navy on September 6, 1940, the Dauntless was powered by a 1,000-horsepower Wright Cyclone engine. Its performance was not very impressive. Underpowered from the very beginning, the speed, range, and load-carrying capability of the Dauntless led many to consider it obsolete. Because of its poor range, the U.S. Navy did not deploy its SBDs aboard its carriers. The first 57 production aircraft went to the U.S. Marines. When the Japanese struck Pearl Harbor, three squadrons were equipped with the SBD-2 Dauntless.

The first truly combat-worthy Dauntless was the SBD-3 model. For the first two years of the Pacific war it would carry much of the U.S. Navy's offensive burden. In the U.S. Army Air Force, the Dauntless was given the name "Banshee" and designated A-24. Serving with the 27th Bombardment Group at New Guinea and with the 351st Fighter Bomber Squadron at Makin, the A-24 suffered heavy casualties and was quickly withdrawn from frontline service.

On May 7, 1942, Dauntless dive bombers from the USS carriers *Lexington* and *Yorktown* sank the Japanese carrier *Shoho*. While the U.S. Navy lost the *Lexington*, the battle of Coral Sea was considered a tactical victory for the Japanese and a strategic one for the United States. It was the first major failure in Japanese plans for conquest and the first of many victories for the Dauntless. A few weeks later, on June 4, 1942, the underpowered Dauntless would again play a major role in victory. The Battle of Midway turned the tide and ended all hopes of Japanese dominance in the Pacific. In the ferocious day-long battle, the U.S. Navy lost the USS *Yorktown* and 109 U.S. carrier aircraft were shot down or ditched due to lack of fuel. The Dauntless was credited with four Japanese carriers and a heavy cruiser sunk. It was an overwhelming victory for the U.S. Navy.

Although the Dauntless was underpowered and tiresome to fly, it was a forgiving machine and a very accurate dive bomber. Dive-bombing missions took place between 15,000 and 20,000 feet (4,570 and 6,095 m). As the pilot approached the target, he would place his machine directly overhead, pull up the nose, deploy upper and lower dive flaps, and push over. Acceleration was slow, and using the Mk VIII reflector sight (replacing the telescope sight on the SBD-5), the pilot would literally point his aircraft at the target and drop his bombs. Free of its heavy bomb load, the Dauntless pulled out quite easily. The aircraft handled well in normal flight, and visibility from the cockpit was excellent. For all its faults, the Dauntless was a tough, reliable machine, and was able to sustain severe battle damage.

Foreign users of the Dauntless included the Royal New Zealand Air Force and Free French Navy. Production of the Dauntless ceased in July 1944, but it would remain the primary U.S. Navy shipboard dive bomber until late 1944.

LEFT: PRE-WAR COLOURS. THIS SBD-1 WOULD SOON LOSE ITS COLOURFUL PAINT SCHEME IN FAVOUR OF LOW-VISIBILITY
GREY-TONE CAMOUFLAGE. *ABOVE*: SBD-3S BEGIN THEIR BOMB RUN ON ENIWETOK.

THE PILOT'S
P E R S P E C T I V E
TOM GREGORY
LONE STAR FLIGHT MUSEUM

When I first sat in the Dauntless cockpit it looked and felt a bit dated. Compared to some of the more modern aircraft I've flown, such as the F4U-5, the Dauntless cockpit seems particularly antiquated. It's a big cockpit that is easy to get in and out of.

The view through the canopy is fair to good, but it's hampered by the many metal strips and pieces that run through it. The big arch out in front of your head, with the big wet compass on top, is especially aggravating. Looking aft is almost impossible because there's a big piece of armour plate.

The instrument panel is kind of bare. The twin 0.50-calibre machine guns on the left and right side of the instrument panel take up a lot of space. Because of that, the engine instruments are down below the main flight instrument panel. It's a little difficult to see those instruments with the chart table installed, even in the stowed position. The throttle has good friction control, but it's located a little forward. In most pictures of Second World War Dauntless pilots, you can see them leaning forward. That's because the stick is too short, again because of the chart table. The prop control—back aft of the throttle and down low—is good. What's really unique in the Dauntless is the tail hook lever. The tail hook is actuated manually with a long baseball-bat-looking pole on the left side of the pilot seat.

The hydraulic controls for the landing gear, dive brakes, and flaps are on the right-hand side of the cockpit. The flap handle is labelled "L," the landing gear handle "W," and the dive brake is labelled "D." You really had be careful with those controls.

In the 1930s, the Dauntless was top of the line. With that in mind, the cockpit is quite complex.

DOUGLAS A-24B restored
to a SBD-5 DAUNTLESS
LONE STAR FLIGHT MUSEUM, GALVESTON, TEXAS

1. MAGNETIC COMPASS
2. GUNSIGHT
3. TACHOMETER
4. ALTIMETER
5. VOR
6. AIRSPEED INDICATOR
7. DIRECTIONAL GYRO
8. MANIFOLD PRESSURE GAUGE
9. ARTIFICIAL HORIZON
10. TURN AND BANK INDICATOR
11. RATE OF CLIMB INDICATOR
12. .50 CALIBRE MACHINE GUNS
13. FUEL QUANTITY GAUGE
14. CYLINDER HEAD TEMP INDICATOR
15. SUCTION GAUGE
16. AUTO PILOT OIL PRESSURE GAUGE
17. OUTSIDE AIR TEMP GAUGE
18. FUEL OIL PRESSURE GAUGE
19. CONTROL COLUMN
20. LANDING GEAR POSITION INDICATOR
21. ARRESTING HOOK CONTROL
22. IGNITION SWITCH
23. THROTTLE
24. COWL FLAP SWITCH
25. BOMB SELECTOR CONTROL
26. FUEL TANK SELECTOR CONTROL

SBD-4 SKIMS OVER LOW-HANGING CLOUDS.

JAPAN

MITSUBISHI ZERO-SEN   MITSUBISHI KI-46-III
                                  "DINAH"

KAWANISHI SHIDEN-KAI   KAWASAKI KI-100-I-OTSU

MITSUBISHI A6M
ZERO-SEN

THE ZERO-SEN WAS THE FIRST CARRIER FIGHTER
CAPABLE OF OUTFLYING LAND-BASED OPPONENTS.

When aircraft designer Jiro Horikoshi received the Imperial Japanese Navy's requirement for a new fighter, he could not believe his eyes. The specifications called for maximum speed of more than 311 miles per hour (500 km/h) at an altitude of 13,123 feet (4,000 m). It had to climb to 9,843 feet (3,000 m) in under three and a half minutes, and carry a pair of 20-mm cannons and two machine guns. Endurance was to be 1.2 to 1.5 hours on internal fuel, and this new fighter — with an engine in the 1,000-horsepower range —

had to operate from the deck of a carrier.

The first Zero-Sen flew on April 1, 1939, with a 780-horsepower radial engine. It attained a speed of 304 miles per hour (489 km/h). Before the third and fourth prototypes completed their trials, the JNAF requested the delivery of 15 pre-production models for operational use in China.

The Zero's first success occurred on September 13, 1940. While escorting bombers for an attack on Chungking, the small Zero escort shot down 27 Chinese fighters. No Zeros were lost, and so began the myth of

THE A6M5 TYPE 0 MODEL 52 WAS BUILT IN LARGER NUMBERS THAN ANY OTHER VARIANT OF THE ZERO-SEN.

invincibility that would surround this new fighter well into the early years of the Second World War.

In the following year, the Zero swept through any and all opposition, but because it was fighting a largely forgotten war in China, the new fighter's exploits went mostly unnoticed. Plunged into war on December 7, 1941, American fighter pilots were not prepared for the nimble Zero. Early aircraft losses were horrendous, and the swift Japanese victories helped solidify the Zero's reputation in both American and Japanese minds. Caught completely by surprise, the Allies were astonished at the sight of the new fighter. Reports on the Zero had been prepared before the attack on Pearl Harbor, but they had been ignored. As losses in the Pacific mounted, the U.S. authorities claimed the Zero was a poor copy of existing western designs. Once this was accepted, it then became possible to speak more highly of the Zero.

The first American aircraft to challenge the Zero was the tubby F4F Wildcat. Because of its lighter weight, the Zero had superior speed, acceleration, rate of climb, and manoeuvrability. It was only through the use of dive and zoom tactics and two-plane attacks,

as well the Wildcat's ability to absorb punishment, that the Wildcat was able to redress the balance.

In June 1942, the Japanese suffered their first major defeat. At the Battle of Midway they lost 234 aircraft and four carriers, ending the Zero's effective operation from heavy carriers.

As the war progressed, the Japanese were thrown onto the defensive. New American types, such as the P-38 Lighting, the Corsair, and the Hellcat were introduced, but the Japanese failed to recognize the need for a replacement for the Zero. Effectively, it was the same aircraft that had fought four years earlier, and with newer models coming off the production lines, the Zero could not keep pace. By 1945, the once-victorious Zero was being used for a new cause.

The Kamikaze story has been told many times. The first Kamikazes were launched during the Battle of the Philippines, in October 1944. Although extensive damage was inflicted on the invasion fleet, the outcome was never in doubt. Of the 331 Zeros launched, 158 reached their targets.

Mitsubishi produced a total of 3,879 Zero-Sen fighters, and Nakajima built a further 6,215.

THE PILOT'S
P E R S P E C T I V E

USAAF INFORMATIONAL INTELLIGENCE SUMMARY NO. 59
SEPTEMBER 4, 1942

For some time past, incomplete, confusing, and occasionally conflicting information has prevailed regarding the Japanese Zero Fighter. During recent weeks, examinations and investigations of crashed Zeros in various parts of the world have clarified the situation. For this reason, it is believed that the following detailed summary will prove of interest.

Although perhaps somewhat smaller than average, the cockpit provides ample room for a pilot of normal size. Instruments are conveniently arranged and visibility is good. No automatic flight control apparatus is installed, but the instrument panel contains practically all other flight and navigational instruments found in modern fighters, including artificial horizon, radio compass dial and bank-and-turn indicator. A rudder bar is provided rather than individual rudder pedals. Metal stirrups in hinged toe plates mounted at each end of the bar provide individual brake control, which is obtained through built-in Bowden wire connections to two hydraulic cylinders mounted on the cockpit floor just in front of the rudder bar. The entire rudder bar and fittings are manually adjusted fore and aft by means of a screw to accommodate pilots of different leg length. The control stick is of normal design, but contains neither trigger nor gun selector switches. These are found upon the throttle handle on the left side of the cockpit. A small, rocking thumb lever in the top of the throttle handle selects in the forward position the 7.7s and the 20-mm wing guns. A long, curved trigger is fitted to the forward side of the throttle handle. On the next inner quadrant, slightly below the throttle, a supercharger control lever is mounted. Inboard and slightly below the supercharger handle is the handle for the propeller pitch control. The mixture control handle is mounted on a separate quadrant, slightly higher and forward of the other group.

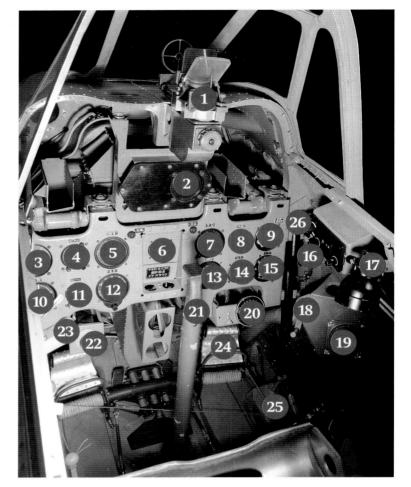

MITSUBISHI ZERO A6M3
FLIGHT MAGIC INC., SANTA MONICA, CALIFORNIA

1. TYPE 98 REFLECTOR GUNSIGHT
2. TURN AND BANK INDICATOR
3. EXHAUST TEMP GAUGE
4. CLOCK
5. AIRSPEED INDICATOR
6. MAGNETIC COMPASS
7. RATE OF CLIMB INDICATOR
8. TACHOMETER
9. FUEL & OIL PRESSURE GAUGE
10. RADIO DIRECTION INDICATOR
11. MAGNETO SWITCH
12. ALTIMETER
13. CYLINDER HEAD TEMP GAUGE
14. "G" METER
15. MANIFOLD PRESSURE
16. DIRECTION FINDER CONTROL UNIT
17. INSTRUMENT LIGHT
18. COWL FLAP CONTROL
19. FRESH AIR DUCT
20. OIL COOLER SHUTTER CONTROL
21. CONTROL COLUMN
22. PRIMER
23. THROTTLE
24. RUDDER PEDAL
25. EMERGENCY GEAR-DOWN LEVER
26. EMERGENCY FUEL PUMP LEVER

TEST FLIGHT OF A CAPTURED A6M5
ZERO TYPE 0 IN THE UNITED STATES.

"DINAH"

CODENAMED "DINAH," ALLIED AIRCREWS CALLED IT THE AIRCRAFT WITH THE NICE "LINAH."

Undoubtedly, the Ki-46 was one of the cleanest and most efficient aircraft to see combat service in the Second World War. Blessed with elegant lines, the Dinah was considered a masterpiece of the Japanese aircraft industry. Fast and reliable, the Ki-46 performed the task of high-altitude reconnaissance with great success. From the beginning of its operational career to the final stages of the War, the Ki-46 was a constant pain in the Allies' side. It was one of the few Japanese aircraft that could penetrate Allied airspace with a good chance of survival. The Dinah's performance was respected by friends and foes alike, and at one time, the Luftwaffe seriously considered building the aircraft under licence!

In 1937, the Japanese Imperial Army was keenly aware of Japan's geographical limitations. Surrounded by vast oceans, the need for a long-range, high-speed reconnaissance aircraft became a top priority. In November 1939, the first flight of the Ki-46 occurred at Kagamigahara, in Gifu Prefecture, north of Nagoya. Powered by two 900-horsepower Mitsubishi Ha-26-I engines, the prototype performed well and obtained a speed of 355 miles per hour (540 km/h) at 13,125 feet (4,000 m). As the flight tests continued, it soon became evident that the Ki-46 would not meet its design speed; it was some 40 miles per hour slower than anticipated. Even with this minor setback, the Army still considered it a good aircraft; compared to the Ki-43-I and the A6M2 single-engine fighters, the Ki-46 was faster and could fly higher.

In March 1941, the K-46-II was completed. It reached a speed of 375 miles per hour (604 km/h) at 19,030 ft (5,800 m). Deliveries soon followed, and in July 1941 the Ki-46-II began to see service in China and Manchuria. The Chinese Air Force did not have a fighter capable of intercepting the speedy, high-flying Ki-46-II. As tensions mounted in the Pacific, and war with the Allies was about to begin, a unit of Ki-46-IIs was moved to French Indo-China in October 1941. Reconnaissance missions were conducted over Malaya in anticipation of the planned amphibious landings. When war finally broke out, the Ki-46-II was deployed in small units and assigned to cover the entire Southeast Asia area. Allied fighters were continually frustrated, and without ground radar control to guide them, they could never hope to intercept the Dinahs. The Ki-46-II flew their missions with almost complete immunity. This performance did not go unnoticed, and the Ki-46-II's performance soon caught the attention of the Japanese Navy, which quickly acquired a small number for use against Northern Australia.

The appearance of the P-38F Lighting and Spitfire Mk V in the South Pacific and the defence of Darwin spelled the end of the Ki-46-II's early success. But the Japanese were one step ahead. In May 1942, Mitsubishi installed their new 1,500-horsepower Ha-112-II engine into an updated version of the aircraft. The Ki-46-III emerged with a speed of 404 miles per hour (650 km/h), a range of 2,485 miles, and a new, more streamlined cockpit and nose section. Able to operate in areas where the Allies had achieved air superiority, the Ki-46-III kept a constant watch on Allied airfields, including the B-29 airfields in the Marianas. Only with ample warning could the fast-climbing Allied fighters hope to intercept the high flying Ki-46-III. But as the War drew to a close, and with Allied air superiority complete, Dinah units began to suffer heavy losses.

When the B-29 appeared over Japan, there were few fighters available with the high-altitude performance required to effectively intercept it. Immediate modifications were incorporated into the Ki-46-III and it was soon turned into the Ki-46-III-KAI Type 100 Air Defence Fighter. Armament included two forward-firing 20-mm cannons and one obliquely mounted forward-firing 37 mm cannon located in the centre fuselage section. In February 1945, the Dinah was still one of the best reconnaissance aircraft of the War.

RIGHT: CAPTURED KI.46-III LONG-RANGE RECONNAISSANCE AIRCRAFT.

THE PILOT'S
P E R S P E C T I V E
ROBERT C. MIKESH
FORMER SENIOR CURATOR OF THE
NATIONAL AIR AND SPACE MUSEUM

This particular model has so much glass in front of it that the distraction in flight would have been something unreal, especially with reflection at night. The pilot would very likely have taken in cockpit fumes on every take-off because the front fuel tank was right in front of the pilot and there was nothing between one's nostrils and the filler cap. Access to this filler port was to the left of the forward canopy, so I can't see how you could have avoided having fumes in the cockpit.

This cockpit is comfortable, and the engines are right out where you can see them, yet do not hinder visibility, as they are set relatively low. The long nose on the Ki-46-III assists in pitch control for the pilot. This being a third-generation cockpit for the Dinah, the instrumentation is good and everything is close to hand. Although designed for high-altitude reconnaissance work, the Ki-46-III did not have cockpit heating as far as I know.

In this Dinah III cockpit, the pilot's sight line is higher than the engines, which means you did not have to drop the wing tip to see straight out. Having said that, they do seem to hinder downward visibility.

Armour protection in the Ki-46-III cockpit was normal and usually consisted of plates fitted in the field. These field retrofits were never as effective as the armour plate that was designed and installed in production.

I rate the cockpit of the Ki-46-III very high for a twin-engine aircraft of that time period. I say that because its narrow single-pilot cockpit is hindered very little by its large-diameter engines.

A CAPTURED KI-46-III IN NEARLY PRISTINE CONDITION.

MITSUBISHI Ki-46-III "DINAH"
AEROSPACE MUSEUM, COSFORD, ENGLAND

1. CONTROL COLUMN
2. FRICTION CONTROL
3. EMERGENCY FUEL PUMP
4. WATER METHANOL CONTROL
5. FUEL MIXTURE CONTROLS
6. MAGNETO
7. HYDRAULIC ACCUMULATOR PRESSURE
8. BRAKE PRESSURE GAUGE
9. FUEL TANK GAUGE
10. FUEL TANK QUANTITY SELECTOR

11. ADI PRESSURE GAUGES
12. RPM SYNCHRONIZER
13. RPM INDICATOR
14. MANIFOLD PRESSURE GAUGE (PORT)
15. MANIFOLD PRESSURE GAUGE (STARBOARD)
16. CLOCK
17. AIRSPEED INDICATOR
18. ARTIFICIAL HORIZON
19. RATE OF CLIMB INDICATOR
20. WATER INJECTION FLOW METER
21. EXHAUST TEMP GAUGE

22. EXHAUST TEMP GAUGE
23. FUEL PRESSURE INDICATOR
24. OIL PRESSURE INDICATOR
25. OIL TEMP GAUGES
26. AUTOPILOT HYDRAULIC PRESSURE INDICATOR
27. FUEL PUMP PRIMER
28. FLAP POSITION INDIATOR
29. HYDRAULIC SYSTEM PRESSURE GAUGE
30. UNDERCARRIAGE CONTROL
31. FLAP CONTROL
32. FUEL TANK SELECTORS
33. RUDDER PEDAL
34. OUTSIDE AIR TEMP GAUGE
35. BRAKE

SHIDEN-KAI

TOO LATE TO MAKE ANY REAL IMPACT, THE KAWANISHI SHIDEN-KAI
WAS CONSIDERED BY JAPANESE AND ALLIED PILOTS TO BE
THE BEST FIGHTER IN THE JAPANESE IMPERIAL NAVY.

The modification of a land-based fighter into a floatplane fighter had many successful examples, including the Nakajima A6M2-N and the Supermarine Spitfire VB and IX floatplanes. But the Kawanishi Shiden-Kai is the only land-based fighter derived from a floatplane fighter. The Kawanishi Kokuki KK flew the first prototype of the 15-*Shi* Kyofu float fighter in August 1942. At the same time, work began on the landplane version. Powered by a 1,990-horsepower Nakajima Homare engine, the new Shiden prototype proved to have

outstanding speed and manoeuvrability. Three more prototypes were completed by the end of July 1943, and in less than a year full production was attained.

When Japan entered the War, both the JNAF and JAAF considered manoeuvrability to be of paramount importance, and speed, armour protection, self-sealing tanks and firepower were sacrificed for lightness and manoeuvrability. In the early stages of the War this philosophy proved effective, but as the War progressed, Japanese pilots demanded greater speed, heavier armament, and protection for the pilot and fuel tanks.

SHIDEN-KAI MODEL 21 FIGHTERS WARM-UP FOR THE FERRY FLIGHT TO YOKOSUKA.

Enter the Shiden. The Shiden Model 11 began service in 1944 and proved to be an excellent fighter despite engine problems and other shortcomings. Japanese pilots soon found the Hellcat to be a relatively easy kill. The Japanese built 1,007 examples of the Model 11.

Although the Shiden Model 11 represented a giant leap for Japanese fighter development, it suffered greatly from its hurried development. Sometimes entire units were rendered non-operational.

The Shiden first appeared in large numbers over the Philippines. The 341st Air Corps arrived at Luzon from Formosa. Despite the performance of their new fighter, Japanese pilots could not cope with the numerically superior Americans. Compared to the Hellcat, the Shiden Model 11 was only 13 miles per hour (21 km/h) slower than the Grumman F6F-3 Hellcat and 23 miles per hour (37 km/h) slower than the F6F-5. Despite its limited success, the Shiden still suffered from serious technical problems.

To address this, Kawanishi redesigned the Shiden Model 11, producing the Shiden-Kai (meaning "Violet Lightning"). Like the Model 11, the Shiden-Kai was ordered off the drawing board. The first prototype flew on December 31, 1943, and was accepted by the JNAF and designated the Shiden 21. Externally, the Shiden-Kai was very different from the Shiden 11. The fuselage was lengthened and refined, the mid-wing was replaced by a low-wing mounting and the vertical tail services were completely redesigned. In the hands of a competent pilot, the Shiden-Kai was considered the best all-round fighter in the Pacific. After the Shiden-Kai was evaluated, the Imperial Japanese Navy assigned the new fighter to the new elite 343rd Kokutai Squadron. Experienced pilots and ground crew were recruited for the squadron and it soon became the best fighter unit of the Imperial Japanese Navy. Responsible for the defence of Shikoku and Kyushu, the 343rd Kokutai battled Superfortresses and P-51 Mustangs from Matsuyama and Iwo Jima. In February 1945, Warrant Officer Kinsuke Muto attacked a formation of 12 Grumman Hellcats. Despite the odds, Muto managed to destroy four Hellcats and forced the rest to scatter. By that time, severe fuel shortages were beginning to curtail flight operations. The fuel that was available was being saved for the anticipated Allied amphibious assault against the Japanese Islands. Thus, in the last few weeks of the War, Shidens spent their last days on the ground.

THE PILOT'S
P E R S P E C T I V E
ROBERT C. MIKESH
FORMER SENIOR CURATOR OF THE
NATIONAL AIR AND SPACE MUSEUM

This was a third-generation single-seat fighter cockpit for Kawanishi, a company better known for its large flying boats. On some small fighter aircraft, it feels as though you're sitting on the cockpit floor. This cockpit, however, feels just right. The interior is roomy and comfortable. This makes getting in and out relatively easy—if that can be said about any Second World War fighter. It is not as roomy as the J2M Jack, but it is larger than the A6M Zero. The 360-degree Perplex canopy provides an excellent all-round view.

The Japanese were never as fastidious as Americans concerning the placement of instruments in functional relationships. The Americans consistently clumped all six of the basic flight instruments in one place. In the case of the N1K2-J, these six flight instruments are right there in front of you. The cockpit is well laid out, with the throttle, propeller pitch, and mixture controls placed comfortably at the left hand. One of the most interesting and unique features in the Shiden-Kai cockpit is the loop railing on the throttle quadrant. The loop consists of a half-inch round tube that rests parallel to the run of the throttles. By putting the cushion of your hand on the loop, it allowed you to tweak the throttle and the prop without have to put your hand down on the vernier.

Compared to other Japanese and American cockpits, the Shiden-Kai falls somewhere in the middle. It is very comfortable, and everything seems to be in the right place.

KAWANISHI N1K2-JA SHIDEN KAI
CHAMPLIN FIGHTER MUSEUM, MESA, ARIZONA

1. CONTROL COLUMN
2. THROTTLE HANDLE
3. MIXTURE CONTROLS
4. WING FUEL TANK GAUGE
5. PORT/AFT FUSELAGE TANK READING SWITCH
6. FUEL CONTROL INDICATOR LIGHT
7. FUSELAGE FUEL TANK GAUGE
8. OXYGEN REGULATOR
9. TACHOMETER
10. EXHAUST THERMOMETER
11. RADIO HOMING INDICATOR
12. SUCTION PRESSURE GAUGE
13. TURN AND BANK INDICATOR
14. AIR SPEED INDICATOR
15. CARBURETTOR AIR TEMP GAUGE
16. CYLINDER HEAD TEMP GAUGE
17. OIL PRESSURE GAUGE
18. ARTIFICIAL HORIZON
19. ALTIMETER
20. WATER/METHANOL PRESSURE GAUGE
21. COCKPIT LIGHT RHEOSTAT KNOB
22. ENGINE MAGNETO SWITCH
23. OIL TEMP GAUGE
24. COMPASS
25. RATE OF CLIMB INDICATOR
26. DUAL ADI INSTRUMENT
27. LANDING GEAR POSITION INDICATOR
28. OIL COOLER DOOR ADJUSTMENT
29. PROPELLER ANTI-ICING FLUID PUMP
30. EMERGENCY HYDRAULIC HAND PUMP
31. COWL FLAP ADJUSTMENT CRANK
32. CARBURETTOR INTAKE DOOR
33. FRESH AIR VENT
34. ENGINE FUEL PRIMER PUMP
35. GUNSIGHT

SHIDEN N1K1-J MODEL 11 IN THE PHILIPPINES.

Ki-100

AT LOW AND MEDIUM ALTITUDES, THE KI-100 WAS SUPERB AND POTENTIALLY THE MASTER OF ALL FIGHTER OPPONENTS.

In March 1945, a new and potent interceptor fighter began operations over the Japanese home islands. This new fighter outperformed the F6F Hellcat and would prove its equal to the formidable P-51D Mustang. Not found in any Allied recognition manuals, the Kawasaki Ki-100 came as a definite shock. No one expected to see such a new and advanced fighter at this stage of the War. The Allies' assessments were only half correct. The new Ki-100 was not an entirely new aircraft, but it was the work of supreme engineering improvisation. At the end of 1945, 275 Ki-61 Hien (Tony) airframes sat awaiting engines. There was little or no hope of these aircraft ever receiving their in-line liquid-cooled engines, and at this point the Japanese were desperate for aircraft.

With such an abundance of Ki-61 Hien airframes, the Japanese decided to fit a radial engine to the existing airframes. They chose the Mitsubishi Ha-112-II large-diameter radial. Adapting an airframe designed for one type of engine to accept another was a formidable task. Only two other fighters, the radial-engine Fw 190 and the Lavochkin LaGG-3, were re-engined successfully (the Fw 190 was adapted to take an in-line power plant to become the superb Fw 190D, and the LaGG-3 received a radial powerplant, creating the La-5).

The Ki-100 was a remarkable engineering achievement, and after just seven weeks, on February 1, 1945, the first prototype took to the air. Peformance results were better than expected. Matched against a captured P-51C, the Ki-100 was slower but enjoyed a distinct advantage in manoeuvrability and possessed superior diving characteristics. It was concluded that with pilots of equal skill, the Ki-100 should emerge victorious. The Ki-100 excelled at low and medium altitudes and was better than anything the Allies had, except for the P-51D, which did not appear until May 1945. Above 23,000 feet (7,000 m), performance deteriorated quickly. Armed with two 20-mm Ho-5 cannons and two 12.7-mm Ho-103 machine guns, the Ki-100 carried a respectable punch.

The Ki-100 was popular with ground crews, and at this late stage of the War it was considered the most reliable aircraft in the Japanese inventory. As fast as the Hien airframes could be fitted with the new engine, the Ki-100 was issued to new fighter squadrons. The 18th Sentai was the first unit to see action with the new type, but it was the 244th Sentai that became the first unit to be exclusively equipped with the new type. The 244th enjoyed great success in fighter-versus-fighter combat, and on June 3, 1945, the unit claimed the destruction of seven F4U Corsairs. On July 25, the 244th Sentai attacked a superior force of F6F Hellcats claiming 12 kills.

A marriage of convenience, the mating of the Ki-61 Hien airframe with the Ha-112-II engine proved to be a wonderful success. The 500 Ki-100s that were produced obtained an enviable combat record, despite the numerical superiority of the Allies and the critical shortage of trained pilots. When compared to other fighter developments, which in some cases took years, the Ki-100's remarkable lifespan, from conception to final demise, covered just 10 months!

In *Air International*, October 1976, Masashi Sumita, a former 18th Sentai pilot compared the P-51D with the Ki-100: "In my view, the Ki-100 was capable of taking on two Mustangs at one time. Its turning capability was such that there was no problem in shaking a Mustang from one's tail. The engine of the Ki-100 was excellent, and in my opinion the Kawasaki fighter suffered only two serious defects: the fuses of the electrical gun-operating mechanism were prone to blowing, and the radio equipment was virtually useless in many circumstances."

RIGHT: LINE-UP OF CAPTURED KI-100S. INSET: KI-100-I-OTSU IN SERVICE WITH THE 5TH SENTAI IN DEFENCE OF THE NAGOYA AREA.

THE PILOT'S
PERSPECTIVE
ROBERT C. MIKESH
FORMER SENIOR CURATOR OF THE NATIONAL AIR AND SPACE MUSEUM

T he Ki-100-IIb model had the factory-formed fuselage rather than the modified Ki-61-II airframe. It had a smaller cockpit than most radial-engine aircraft because it was designed as a slender, in-line-engine fighter.

The cockpit instrumentation and layout is on par with the George. Although the tip of the instrument panel sits higher in the Ki-100, it makes you feel like you're sitting lower in the cockpit, which gives you less visibility. The one thing you had to look out for in the Ki-100 cockpit was the fuel selector valve, located just behind your left heel. I would have been very uncomfortable with that, for fear of inadvertently kicking it and starving the engine of fuel.

One of the strangest things in the Ki-100 is the wobble pump, which is used to pump starting fuel to the engine. Instead of actually rocking the pump lever, you had to push and pull this poker handle that was hinged to the pump handle.

Both the methanol and fuel fuselage tanks on the Ki-100, aft left and right, are filled through the cockpit. This is very unusual because in jostling the fuel, you're very likely to get fumes in the cockpit on initial ground operations. Another concern would have been the cordite fumes from the two 12.7-mm machine guns mounted in the cockpit. But all fighters with nose-mounted guns had that problem.

The Ki-100 was reported to be a very docile airplane. The long nose in front gave an early indication of any oscillation, and the wide-track landing gear made it very stable on take-off and landing.

KAWASAKI Ki-100-IIB
AEROSPACE MUSEUM, COSFORD, ENGLAND

1. CONTROL COLUMN
2. THROTTLE HANDLE
3. PROPELLER PITCH CONTROL
4. ENGINE MAGNETO SWITCH
5. TACHOMETER
6. OIL TEMP GAUGE
7. TURN AND BANK INDICATOR

8. METHANOL PRESSURE GAUGE
9. AIR SPEED INDICATOR
10. RATE OF CLIMB INDICATOR
11. COOLANT FLAP GAUGE
12. LANDING FLAP POSITION INDICATOR

13. FUEL TANK READING SELECTOR SWITCH
14. ENGINE FUEL PRIMER PUMP
15. CLOCK
16. FUEL TANK SELECTOR SWITCH
17. GUNSIGHT MOUNT
18. COWL FLAP POSITION INDICATOR

KI-100S OF THE 5TH SENTAI SHORTLY BEFORE THE END OF THE WAR.

U.S.S.R.

Yakovlev Yak-3

YAKOVLEV
YAK-3

LUFTWAFFE FIGHTER PILOTS WERE TOLD TO "AVOID COMBAT BELOW FIVE THOUSAND METRES WITH YAKOVLEV FIGHTERS LACKING AN OIL COOLER INTAKE BENEATH THE NOSE!"

By 1944, the Soviet aeronautical industry was fully recovered and was producing fighters and bombers at a prodigious rate. As a result of the massive reorganizing that began in 1941–42, the Soviets were able to produce 35,000 aircraft in 1943 and 40,300 in 1944. In all, the Soviets produced 125,000 aircraft, just over half of which were single-seat fighters of the famous Yakovlev series.

The Yak-1 first appeared in 1941. By 1942, the Yakovlev design bureau began work on a high-performance light fighter capable of maintaining aerial superiority over the battlefield. Smaller than the Yak-1, the Yak-3 was powered by an M-105PF-2 engine rated at 1,222 horsepower. The wing span was reduced, an all-round vision cockpit canopy was fitted, and the oil cooler intake was transferred to the port wing root. Performance figures were impressive. The Yak-3 was superior to early versions of the Yak-9 and attained a maximum speed of 403 miles per hour (649 km/h) at 16,400 feet (5,000 m). The handling characteristics were described as "excellent," and pilots who flew both the Spitfire and the Yak claimed that the Yak-3 was lighter on the ailerons and smoother to fly.

Impressive as these figures were, the Yak-3 had a relatively high stalling speed, and take-off and landing could be a problem with novice pilots. Armament was light: one 20-mm cannon with 120 rounds and two 12.7-mm machine guns with 250 rounds per gun.

The operational debut of the Yak-3 occurred during the German offensive at Kursk in August 1943. This would be the last German offensive in the East. From that point on, the initiative switched to the Soviets. By spring 1944, several VVS fighter regiments were equipped with the Yak-3. The success of the Yak-3 was profound, and German fighter pilots were warned not

to engage the fighter below 16,200 feet (5,000 m). Russian records state that on July 14, 1944, a formation of 8 Yak-3s intercepted a formation of 60 Ju 87 dive bombers and Bf 109Gs. The Yak-3s destroyed three Ju 87s and four Bf 109s without loss. The following day, 18 Yak-3s engaged 30 Luftwaffe fighters, destroying 15 for a loss of one. In the summer of 1944, the French Normandie-Niemen Group reportedly choose the Yak-3 over other Russian fighters and Lend-Lease American and British aircraft. A considerable number of their 273 victories were obtainedwhile flying the Yak-3

In terms of manoeuvrability, the Yak-3 was outstanding, proving itself more agile than the Bf 109G and Fw 190A below 20,000 feet (6,000 m). The Yak-3 was used in many roles, including ground attack, bomber escort, and low-altitude interceptor.

In early 1944, the M-107A engine was installed in a Yak-3 airframe. Powered by this new engine, the Yak-3 attained a speed of 447 miles per hour (719 km/h) at 18,865 feet (5,750 m) and proved to be 60 to 70 miles per hour (97 to to 113 km/h) faster than the Bf 109G-2 and Fw 190A-4. The official report concluded that the M-107A-powered Yak-3 "appears to offer the best performance of all indigenous and known foreign fighters, being superior in horizontal speed, rate of climb and manoeuvrability." Production began in late 1944, but that was too late for the version to see action.

Compared to western fighters, the Yak-3 lacked firepower and its altitude performance was poor. But these faults were minor considering its excellent stability under all flying conditions, its good controllability at high angles of attack, and its pleasant handling characteristics.

ABOVE: LIGHTER ON THE AILERONS AND SMOOTHER TO FLY THAN THE SPITFIRE, THE YAK-3 WAS AN EXCEPTIONAL PERFORMER AT LOW AND MEDIUM ALTITUDES. *RIGHT*: PILOTS MAN THEIR PLANES. THE YAK-3 MADE ITS COMBAT DEBUT DURING THE BATTLE OF KURSK IN AUGUST 1943.

THE PILOT'S
PERSPECTIVE
STEPHEN GREY
THE FIGHTER COLLECTION

The Yak-3 was a Central European airplane. Most Europeans would have felt reasonably comfortable in the cockpit. Like the Spitfire and the Hurricane, it had air brakes on the control column.

The Yak-3 has a German-style gun button and German-style cocked handle (off at an angle, so that when you pull you don't actually have to adjust your hand). The average Brit would have said that this wasn't a serious requirement, because you might need two hands in some circumstances, but I think you could have used two hands in this thing.

It's a small, tight cockpit for big man, but it's pretty good in ergonomic terms. You have an air control at the back, a gear control on the throttle side, and a throttle and prop link that you could operate together if you wished. The elevator trim is poorly place, and was probably something of an afterthought.

On the control panel, you had the usual speed indicator, compass, slip-and-turn, and rate-of-climb, but no artificial horizon. Down the right-hand side you've got your engine instruments, oil temperature gauge, coolant gauge, and a boost gauge. The gunsight is in the middle, similar to British fighter cockpits of the period.

The Yak-3 packed a lot of power into a very small airframe, and it could turn and roll like crazy. When flown by very determined Russian and French pilots, it was quite a threat. I think it is typical of Russian fighters. Everything is robust, simple, and extremely effective, but it requires a high skill level to fly.

NORMANDIE-NIEMEN PILOTS PREFERRED THE YAK-3 TO EITHER THE YAK-1 OR YAK-9.

YAKOVLEV YAK-3
OLD FLYING MACHINE COMPANY, DUXFORD, ENGLAND

1. AIR SYSTEM PRESSURE
2. LANDING GEAR LEVER
3. "G" METER
4. ALTIMETER
5. AIRSPEED INDICATOR
6. BOOST GAUGE
7. COMPASS
8. TURN AND BANK INDICATOR
9. RPM
10. VSI
11. FUEL, OIL PRESSURE & OIL TEMP GAUGE
12. FUEL GAUGE
13. GENERATOR SWITCH
14. VOLT METER
15. COOLANT TEMP GAUGE
16. EMERGENCY GEAR LOWER HANDLE
17. THROTTLE
18. GUNSIGHT
19. MIXTURE CONTROLS
20. CONTROL COLUMN
21. GUN BUTTON
22. AIR BRAKE
23. TRIM WHEEL
24. RUDDER PEDALS

GERMANY

MESSERSCHMITT BF 109

FOCKE WULF FW 190

JUNKERS JU 87

MESSERSCHMITT ME 410

MESSERSCHMITT ME 163

MESSERSCHMITT ME 262

MESSERSCHMITT
Bf 109

WONDERFULLY VERSATILE AND A COLOSSAL SUCCESS,
THE BF 109 WAS PRODUCED IN GREATER NUMBERS
THAN ANY OTHER FIGHTER AIRCRAFT (OVER 30,000 PRODUCED).

In the summer of 1935, the Luftwaffe began an ambitious expansion program. Its first priority was to acquire a new fighter to replace the obsolete Heinkel He 51, so a requirement was issued for a single-seat monoplane fighter. A gifted young designer by the name of Willy Messerschmitt accepted the challenge and produced an all-metal stressed-skin monoplane fighter with enclosed cockpit, streamlined airframe, and retractable undercarriage. The prototype flew in 1935, and in 1937 the first production model the Bf 109B-1 entered service. For the next eight years the Bf 109 would serve the Luftwaffe in almost every capacity, including interceptor, fighter-bomber, night-fighter, photo-reconnaissance, escort fighter, and ground attack. Produced in greater numbers than any other type, it would be the mainstay of the German Fighter Arm.

At the outbreak of the Second World War, the Bf 109 ruled the skies over Europe. For nearly a year, the Allies were hard pressed to match its performance. RAF Hurricanes and early model Spitfires were easily handled, as were the Curtiss Hawk 75, Morane-Saulneir 406 and Dewotine D 520 of the French Air Force. The Battle of Britain would prove to be the Bf 109E's first real test. The battle began with attacks on coastal shipping in July 1940. Unprepared for long-range escort, the strengths and weaknesses of the Bf 109E soon became apparent. Both the Hurricane and Spitfire could out-turn the Bf109E below 15,000 feet (4,600 m). Above 20,000feet (6,100 m) the Bf 109E was faster than the Spitfire and Hurricane. The Bf 109's greatest shortcoming was its range. When flying bomber escort or *freijagd* ("free hunt") sweeps over southern England, the Bf 109E could fly as far as London, but would only have 20 minutes fighting time over the target.

In the spring of 1941, the Bf 109E was replaced by the new and more effective Bf 109F Friedrich. Deliveries coincided with deliveries of the Mark V Spitfire, thus maintaining a qualitative balance. It was in mid-1942 that the Bf 109 encountered a new, more formidable threat. American B-17s and B-24s began bombing attacks in France and the Low Countries. Downing one of these four-engine bombers required at least 20 hits with 20-mm explosive shells. The Bf 109F's fuselage mounted battery of one 20-mm cannon and two 7.9-mm machine guns proved wholly inadequate. A field modification kit was issued consisting of two 151/20-mm cannons with 120 rounds each. These were mounted under the wings, outboard of the propeller disc. The additional armament trebled the firepower, but general performance and handling suffered.

The year 1943 saw a sharp increase in the number of U.S. daylight attacks on German targets. Fighter units from all fronts were pulled back to defend the homeland. These units soon received the new Bf 109G Gustav series. The G series would be built in greater numbers than any other variant. In spring 1944, American escort fighters joined the battle in strength. P-38s, P-47s and the long-range P-51 Mustangs attacked the German Fighter Arm in the air and on the ground. Between January and April 1944, the Luftwaffe lost 1,000 pilots.

The final version of the Bf 109 to see service in the Second World War was the Bf 109K Kurfurst. The final sub-type was the K-14, powered by the DB605L engine with two-stage supercharger, giving it a top speed of 452 miles per hour (727 km/h).

LEFT: BF109G-6 WITH STANDARD ARMAMENT OF ONE 20MM CANNON THROUGH THE PROPELLER AND TWO 13MM MACHINE GUNS OVER THE ENGINE. *ABOVE*: A BF 109G-5 ON A BOMBER ESCORT MISSION OVER THE ADRIATIC.

THE PILOT'S
P E R S P E C T I V E
PAUL DAY
SQUADRON LEADER
BATTLE OF BRITAIN MEMORIAL FLIGHT
TRANSCRIPT FROM THE DOCUMENTARY *SPITFIRE*.

Entering the only airworthy original wartime Bf 109G for the first time, Paul is immediately struck by its cramped confines. "The overall impression is actually most discouraging. The second immediate impression is just how unbelievably small it is. It's probably a good 25 percent less working room even than a Spitfire. There is actually no room whatsoever. In fact, I could do with a lot more room at shoulder height. There is quite considerable interference with the ability to move the stick left and right. It affects your ability to swivel 'round, even without the canopy shut."

Paul closes the heavy, square-framed canopy. "Well, well. This certainly isn't for the squeamishly claustrophobic. Even with no helmet and with a relatively low seat cushion my head is already against the top of the canopy. The view forward is almost all either Krupp of Essen or 2 inches of armoured glass. It's impossible to fly this airplane with the canopy open, which tends for the provision of the sliding side windows.

"To be fair to the airplane, there are some features in the cockpit which I actually like. Starting on the left, the elevator trim wheel is perhaps a bit too big, but nicely positioned and businesslike. The throttle quadrant is nice, throttle friction is nice, it's all businesslike, well-to-hand, and, of course, that allows sufficient space for what is perhaps the best comparative feature cockpitwise between the 109 and Spit, in that the undercarriage controls are nicely to hand just in front of the throttle controls and they do not require that one changes hands immediately after take-off. Blind flying panel looks okay and I particularly like the artificial horizon. One can cage it and thereby keep it from damage.

"The engine gauges, fuel gauge, quite reasonably easy to read, but other than that it is unbelievably small, unbelievably cramped, and I certainly wouldn't want to go to war in it."

A PILOT PREPARES FOR ANOTHER FLIGHT
IN HIS PRISTINE Bf 109E-7, SICILY.

MESSERSCHMITT Bf 109G-2TROP
IMPERIAL WAR MUSEUM, DUXFORD, ENGLAND

1. CONTROL COLUMN	7. ALTIMETER	15. WINDSCREEN DE-ICE VALVE
2. GUN BUTTON	8. AIRSPEED INDICATOR	16. RUDDER PEDAL
3. REPEATER COMPASS	9. TACHOMETER	17. STARBOARD RADIATOR ISOLATION HANDLE
4. ARTIFICIAL HORIZON	10. PROPELLER PITCH INDICATOR	18. RADIATOR FLAPS OPERATING SWITCH
5. MANIFOLD PRESSURE GAUGE	11. TEMP GAUGE, COOLANT AND OIL	19. OXYGEN REGULATOR
6. ELECTRIC SOCKET FOR REVI GUN SIGHT	12. FUEL CONTENTS GAUGE	20. CLOCK
	13. PRESSURE GAUGE, FUEL AND OIL	21. THROTTLE LEVER
	14. UNDERCARRIAGE EMERGENCY LOWERING HANDLE	22. INSTRUMENT PANEL LIGHT
		23. CIRCUIT BREAKERS
		24. FIRING DOLLS-EYE FOR STARBOARD UNDERWING MG 151
		25. EXTERNAL STORES JETTISON HANDLE

FOCKE WULF
Fw 190

ALTHOUGH IT LACKED THE ELEGANT LINES OF THE SPITFIRE,
THE FW 190 WAS A MASTERPIECE OF DESIGN AND ONE OF THE FINEST
PISTON-ENGINE FIGHTERS OF THE SECOND WORLD WAR.

The Fw 190 was conceived in 1937 as a replacement for the Bf 109. The first pre-production models of the Fw 190A-0 entered service trials in March 1941. Although blessed with superb flying characteristics, the new Fw 190 suffered from chronic engine problems. The BMW 801 engine had a tendency to overheat and was not ready for operational service.

In the summer of 1941, the first combat-ready Fw 190A-1s entered service. Pilots were delighted with their performance, but a number of teething problems remained. The four MG17 7.9-mm machines guns were considered wholly inadequate and were described as "door knockers," and the pair of low-velocity MGFF 20-mm cannons were not well suited for air-to-air combat.

Early British descriptions of the new Fw 190 had it confused with the Curtiss Hawk. It was not until October 1941 that the RAF obtained a gun-camera image of the new fighter. The appearance of the Fw 190 could not have come at a worse time for the RAF. In the previous six months, RAF cross-channel operations had suffered heavy losses. In the latter half of 1941, the RAF lost 411 fighters, compared to a loss of just 103 Luftwaffe fighters. With the advent of the Fw 190, the situation became critical. Equipped with Spitfire V, the RAF was at a distinct disadvantage. The Fw 190 was faster and could outclimb, outdive, and outgun the Spitfire V. Its performance was so superior that Luftwaffe pilots were able to engage and break off combat at will. For the next eight months, the Spitfire squadrons took a beating. It was not until the introduction of the Spitfire IX in July 1942 the balance was redressed.

In August 1942, the Fw 190A-4 was well established in squadron service, with over 200 available for Channel operations. The Fw 190A-4 had been up-gunned, with four 20-mm cannons and two 7.9-mm machine guns. It was also fitted with a new BMW 2,100-horsepower water-injected engine.

During the ill-fated Dieppe raid by Canadian troops in August 1942, Luftwaffe fighters shot down 106 Allied aircraft, including 88 Spitfires. The Luftwaffe lost 20 fighters and 28 bombers. Fw 190 pilots accounted for 97 of the 106 Allied aircraft lost.

As successful as the Focke Wulf Fw 190 was, the changing fortunes of war would soon severely test the Luftwaffe fighter arm. In 1943, American B-17 and B-24 four-engine bombers began bombing targets in Germany. On October 14, 1943, the 8th Air Force suffered horrendous losses when a force of 291 B-17s attacked Regensberg and Schweinfurt, deep inside Germany. At the end of the day, Fw 190s and Bf 109s accounted for 60 shot down and 138 damaged. The Fw 190A was also used in the night-fighter role. As the RAF night-bomber campaign grew, the Luftwaffe turned to the Fw 190. Adapting "wild boar" tactics, Fw 190 pilots would use the glow of searchlights and the fires below to find their targets. Some 200 RAF heavy bombers are believed to have been destroyed during the last half of 1943 using this tactic.

With the advent of the long-range P-47 and P-51 Mustang, the Fw 190's poor high-altitude performance was exposed. Above 20,000 feet (6,096 m) its performance fell off significantly. To improve performance, a radical change was proposed. In place of the BMW air-cooled radial, the Jumo 213A in-line liquid-cooled engine was fitted. In August 1944, after two years of development, the Fw 190D-9 began to pour off the assembly line.

ABOVE: THE INTRODUCTION OF FW 190A DRAMATICALLY IMPROVED THE LUFTWAFFE FIGHTER ARM. *RIGHT*: PREPARING FOR TAKE-OFF, AN FW 190A-4 WARMS UP WHILE THE PILOT CHECKS THE ENGINE OIL TEMPERATURE. *RIGHT INSET*: AN FW 190D DODGES A STICK OF BOMBS.

THE PILOT'S
PERSPECTIVE

FROM BRITISH TOP SECRET TECHNICAL REPORT NO. 2075

It is evident that the Fw 190 bears a stronger superficial resemblance to the American Vultee Vanguard A48A than to the Dutch Koolhoven FK or French Bloch 158. It must be inferred, however, that the aircraft is a "copy" of the previous type; on the contrary, it represents a major technical advance over earlier radial-engine fighters.

The cockpit is roomy and well laid out, a special feature being that all instruments and controls are cased in so that only the dials and operating levers or knobs are visible and available.

The front panel is in two parts, the top containing the primary flying and engine instruments. The cut-out switches for all electrical circuits are housed under hinged flaps on the starboard side. The throttle lever and the switches and indicators for the electric operation of undercarriage, flaps and tail incidence, are situated on the port side. The control column is of the Argus type, as used on all German fighters, with a selector switch and firing button for guns and send/receive button for wireless. The guns are fired by means of a button on the front of the control column. There are round counters for each gun, in the cockpit, and a reflector sight, type Revi 12-D is used.

The top line of the fuselage coaming extends into the cockpit and over the instrument panel in the form of a hood through which the screen of the reflector sight protrudes. The instruments are lit up by two lamps, one at each side of this hood.

The Plexiglas cockpit cover is well shaped and carried far back along the fuselage. The greater distance between the engine and the cockpit is particularly striking. The front fixed portion contains a bullet-proof windscreen. The cockpit is comfortable except for lack of head and shoulder room. Ventilation is adequate and fumes are negligible.

FOCKE-WULF Fw 190D-9
USAF MUSEUM, DAYTON, OHIO

1. CONTROL COLUMN
2. BOMB RELEASE BUTTON
3. GUN BUTTON
4. FuG 16ZY RECEIVER FINE TUNING
5. FuG 16ZY VOLUME CONTROL
6. UNDERCARRIAGE CONTROL LAMPS
7. UNDERCARRIAGE AND LANDING FLAP ACTUATION BUTTONS
8. HORIZONTAL STABILIZER TRIM SWITCH
9. THROTTLE LEVER
10. HORIZONTAL STABILIZER TRIM INDICATOR
11. FuG 25A, IFF CONTROL UNIT
12. FUEL SELECTOR LEVER
13. MANUAL UNDERCARRIAGE LOWER HANDLE
14. COCKPIT VENTILATION KNOB
15. ALTIMETER
16. AIRSPEED INDICATOR
17. AMMUNITION COUNTERS
18. ARTIFICIAL HORIZON
19. GUNSIGHT MOUNTING
20. REPEATER COMPASS
21. RATE OF CLIMB INDICATOR
22. VENTRAL STORES MANUAL RELEASE HANDLE
23. FUEL AND OIL PRESSURE GAUGE
24. COOLANT TEMP GAUGE
25. OIL TEMP GAUGE
26. PROPELLER PITCH INDICATOR
27. FUEL GAUGE
28. RUDDER PEDAL
29. SUPERCHARGER PRESSURE GAUGE
30. TACHOMETER
31. OXYGEN FLOW INDICATOR
32. OXYGEN PRESSURE

FW 190 PILOT PREPARES HIS AIRCRAFT FOR TAKE-OFF

JUNKERS
Ju 87

ITS REPUTATION WAS LEGENDARY. THE JU 87 "STUKA"
SANK MORE SHIPS THAN ANY OTHER AIRCRAFT TYPE AND IT STRUCK TERROR
INTO THE HEARTS OF CIVILIANS AND SEASONED TROOPS ALIKE.

In 1933, plans for the new Luftwaffe were beginning to take shape. New aircraft were needed and there were many who considered the dive bomber to be the ideal weapon for close support of the ground forces. The first Ju 87 prototype was powered by a Rolls-Royce Kestrel engine and flew in the spring of 1935.

The Ju 87 began its career in the skies over Spain. In autumn 1936, General Franco's Nationalists asked for German assistance. In combat, the Ju 87 proved to be extremely rugged and relatively easy to handle, but more importantly, its diving characteristics were excellent. The Ju 87 could dive almost vertically and drop its bombs with pinpoint accuracy. After its successful debut in Spain, production orders were increased.

By August 1939, nine *Stukagruppen* were equipped with the Ju 87B model. The usual bomb load for the Ju 87B consisted of one 1,100-pound (500 kg) bomb resting on crutches that swung out from the belly to clear the bomb from the propeller arch. It was common practice to attach sirens —"Trumpets of Jericho"— to the landing gear struts. The noise created by the sirens proved very effective and is the signature sound associated with the Ju 87 Stuka.

Under the protection of fighters, the Ju 87 was very successful. In the first two years of the War, the Stuka flew with relative impunity. It was not until August 1940, during the Battle of Britain, that the Stuka began to show its vulnerability. Facing a determined and organized fighter force, Ju 87 losses mounted. Between August 13 and 18, 41 Ju 87s were shot down. On August 19, they were withdrawn from the battle.

Obsolete before the War started, the Ju 87, like many other Luftwaffe types, was kept in production due to the lack any real replacement. In 1941, the Ju 87 was improved with a new engine, and the airframe was refined to reduce drag. The Ju 87 D Dora could carry a much heavier bomb load, and armament was increased to two 20-mm cannons mounted in the wings and a pair of 7.92-mm machine guns for the rear gunner. By the time the Dora entered service in February 1942, it could do little to sustain its fearsome reputation. Allied fighters ruled out daylight operations, and it was only in areas where the Luftwaffe had gained local air superiority that the Stuka could operate without heavy losses.

Despite Allied air superiority, the Ju 87 managed to find a new role over the Eastern Front. To help combat the increasing number of Russian tanks, the Stuka was fitted with two 37-mm cannons. The new Ju 87 G "flying tank destroyer" was flown by Hans-Ulrich Rudel, whose personal score reached 519 Russian armoured vehicles destroyed. In exchange for that high score, Udel was shot down 30 times, but never by fighters.

In its last operational role, the Stuka was relegated to the night harassment role. Remarkably, the slow-flying Ju 87 proved highly effective. Its low cruising speeds made it easy for the Ju 87 to avoid attacks by Allied night-fighters. Operating only in periods of moonlight, the usual targets were troop concentrations, railway stations, and road transport. Once the target was located, the leader would drop flares to illuminate the area and the attack would commence.

Ironically, the Luftwaffe's reliance on the Ju 87 in 1945 had not changed since the spring of 1940. The last known night ground-attack operation in the West occurred on May 4, 1945. In the East, Hans-Ulrich Rudel sortied for one last tank-hunting flight on May 8, 1945. At the end of the War, no more than 200 Ju 87s were left.

ABOVE: A FULLY LOADED JU 87D-3 OVER THE RUSSIAN FRONT. *RIGHT*: JU 87D-1 OF 7/ST.G 1 PREPARES TO LAND, SUMMER 1942.
INSET: A STUKA PILOT STRAPS HIMSELF IN. NOTE THE WING-MOUNTED MACHINE GUN IN THE FOREGROUND.

THE PILOT'S
P E R S P E C T I V E
D.H. CLARKE
"I was Scared in the Stuka,"
Aeroplane Magazine (wartime issue)

The rumble of the Jumo 211J engine, when I started up, retained a little of its ferocity as though it could remember past victories; but the husky growl of old age can never imitate the snarl of aggression, and the fuselage rattled and shook from the rough running.

The cockpit was roomy and the visibility all round was excellent—there was even a Perspex panel in the floor so that the pilot could view the target through his legs. I failed to see the point of this refinement. After many dive-bombing experiences in Skuas and Kittyhawks, the only method I knew of going down was to put the target under one wing and then peel over and aim directly at it—but perhaps the Germans had a different technique.

Fancy coloured lines were painted around the inside of the windscreen and the hood and marked in degrees. Obviously they were for the pilot to line against the horizon and thereby know the angle of his dive—but what good did that do him? Usually you had enough worries trying to keep the nose pointed at the target, without bothering about judging the angle!

The takeoff was longer than I thought it would be, and it seemed strange not to have an undercarriage to retract. The climb was laborious.

A Kittyhawk, pre-arranged, darted out of the sun and I turned to meet it, clawing for height and aiming just under its belly as I had done so many times against 109s. But the Stuka could not hold the angle, shuddered, stalled, and fell into a dive. It was like flying brick.

I was shot down a dozen times that morning. My opponent was only a clapped-out P-40, so against a Spitfire or a Hurricane there would only be one answer—there only ever was one answer!

JUNKERS Ju 87G-2
RAF Museum, Hendon, England

1. WATER COOLER FLAPS OPERATING BUTTONS
2. ALTIMETER
3. REPEATER COMPASS
4. COOLER FLAP POSITION INDICATOR
5. RADIO ALTIMETER
6. TURN AND BANK INDICATOR
7. AIRSPEED INDICATOR
8. REVCOUNTER (RPM)
9. RADIO NAVIGATION INDICATOR (AFN)
10. RATE OF CLIMB INDICATOR
11. BOOST PRESSURE INDICATOR
12. FUEL CONTENTS GAUGE
13. FUEL/OIL PRESSURE GAUGE
14. OIL TEMP INDICATOR
15. COOLANT TEMP GAUGE
16. RADIO SWITCH PANEL
17. STARTER
18. PROPELLER PITCH CONTROL
19. THROTTLE
20. GUN BUTTON
21. TARGET VIEW PANEL CONTROL FLAP
22. TARGET VIEW PANEL
23. CONTROL COLUMN
24. RUDDER PEDAL
25. SEAT UP/DOWN LEVER

JU 87B-1 WITH LONG-RANGE TANKS.

MESSERSCHMITT
Me 410

ALTHOUGH NOT AS VERSATILE AS THE DE HAVILLAND MOSQUITO,
THE ME 410 WAS A FORMIDABLE AIRCRAFT
AND PROVED TO BE ONE OF THE BEST TWIN-ENGINE
FIGHTER-BOMBERS OF THE SECOND WORLD WAR.

Plans for the Me 210 began in 1937. The Bf 110 was still considered an important aircraft, but a replacement for the Bf 110 would eventually be needed. In 1938, Messerschmitt's proposal was accepted, and work on the Me 210 prototype began. On September 5, 1939, a few days after the start of the Second World War, the Me 210 prototype took to the air.

The first reports were not good. The new aircraft displayed very poor flying characteristics, with dangerous lateral and longitudinal stability. This reality was a huge setback. From the outset, the Me 210 had been designed to fill the long-range fighter, ground-attack, dive-bombing and reconnaissance roles. As flight tests and trials continued, a production order for 1,000 Me 210As was issued.

By the end of 1941, the Me 210 was still not ready for combat. Despite the obvious shortcomings, production continued. In March 1942, modifications were implimented to rectify the Me 210's poor flying performance. The rear fuselage was lengthened and the wing fitted with leading edge slots. The results were dramatic. The modifications were incorporated almost immediately and the new aircraft was designated the Me 410.

The Me 410 introduced several new and unique design features. The pilot sat right up front. The armament was located under the floor of the pilot instead of in front, as on the Bf 110. Underneath the pilot was a spacious bomb bay with room for two 1,102-pound (500 kg) bombs. The forward armament consisted of two 20-mm Mauser MG 151/20 cannons and two 7.92-mm MG17 machine guns. An advanced rear defensive armament was also added, consisting of a large drum mounted in the fuselage, just aft of the wing. On either side of the drum, single 13-mm MG131 machine guns were mounted. These guns were controlled by the observer with an optical gunsight and provided exceptional firepower over the entire rear hemisphere.

In 1944, the Me 410 was well established as an outstanding fighter-bomber. By mid-1944, the Me 410 was committed to the defence of the Reich. Against the unescorted 8th Air Force B-17s and B-24s, the fast and powerful Me 410s were highly effective. Armament was increased to six 20-mm cannons, and some versions carried the 5-cm BK5 cannon. Me 410 operations also included day/night intruder missions over England. On April 2, 1944, about 15 Me 410s successfully shadowed a group of B-24s back to their bases in England. After the bombers landed, the Me 410s attacked, destroying a number of B-24s with a loss of one aircraft. With the arrival of escorting P-51 and P-47 fighters, the Me 410 units began to suffer heavy losses.

By July 1944, the Me 410 began to disappear from operational service. Allied fighters made it impossible for the Me 410 units to operate without suffering horrendous losses. Many units simply disbanded. Production of single-engine fighters took priority, and the manufacture of the Me 410 came to an end. Those aircraft that remained in service were used strictly for reconnaissance flights.

Never as fast or as versatile as the de Havilland Mosquito, the Messerschmitt Me 410 was, nevertheless, a formidable twin-engine fighter-bomber. Production of the Messerschmitt Me 410 reached a total of 1,103 aircraft.

LEFT: THE ME 410 PROVED A CAPABLE COMBAT AIRCRAFT DESPITE ITS TERRIBLE REPUTATION.
INSET: VIEWED FROM THE COCKPIT OF A B-17, AN ME 410 ARMED WITH THE 50-MM BK 6 CANNON BANKS SHARPLY AFTER ITS ATTACK.

THE PILOT'S
P E R S P E C T I V E
FROM "OPERATION OF THE AIRFRAME AND ENGINE INSTALLATION IN THE ME. 410."
SECRET BRITISH REPORT

CREW PREPARATIONS FOR FLIGHT

When the aircraft mechanic reports the aircraft ready for service, climb in, put on parachute, fasten safety belts. Then: **1**. Check setting of seat (adjust seat so that the graticule of the sight is on a level with the eyes, adjust back of seat so that SZK 4, altimeter and arming switch are within easy reach and the control column can be pulled right back); **2**. Connect up wireless helmet, lever on the connection box for plug and socket connection; **3**. Switch on electrical system by means of pull cable (on right); **4**. Switch on 12-amp apparatus for checking undercarriage and landing flaps; **5**. Petrol cocks at "P1" and "P2;" **6**. Switch over fuel tanks to setting 2 (noise of fuel pumps must be audible); **7**. Make sure that the tumbler switch of the fuel tank pump is sealed at "on;" **8**. Set propeller by means of thumb switch to 12 hours, or to 130 hours if aircraft is not loaded; **9**. Place all auxiliary control surfaces at central position; **10**. Compare time, set altimeter and contact altimeter; **11**. If the air is very humid and the temperature below 0 degrees Celsius, switch on pitot tube heating; **12**. Make sure the arming switch is on and the ZSK off. Check oxygen apparatus, as follows: Open valve by two full turns, connect up mask in breathing tubes, and put on. Press knob (right-hand instrument bank, back), oxygen gauge must open lips. Valve remains open during rest of flight; **13**. Open radiator flaps; **14**. Bolt entrance doors; **15**. Start up engines in accordance with Part 2 para 27; **16**. Check pressure oil system by moving landing flaps.

MESSERSCHMITT Me 410A/U2 HORNISSE
AEROSPACE MUSEUM, COSFORD, ENGLAND

1. VERTICAL SPEED INDICATOR
2. TURN AND BANK INDICATOR
3. DOUBLE TACHOMETER
4. ARTIFICIAL HORIZON
5. REPEATER COMPASS
6. GYRO COMPASS
7. OUTSIDE AIR TEMP GAUGE
8. ALTIMETER
9. CONTROL COLUMN
10. GUN BUTTON
11. THROTTLE
12. STARBOARD CONSOLE FRONT REAR: BOMB RELEASE HANDLES, BOMB PATTERN SELECTOR SWITCH AND TEST LAMP, BOMB RELEASE SELECTOR SWITCHES, CIRCUIT TEST LAMPS, OXYGEN FLOW INDICATOR, OXYGEN INDICATOR, FuG 16 CONTROL UNIT, BOMB FUSING PANEL
13. LOWER INSTRUMENT PANEL: PROP PITCH INDICATORS, COOLANT TEMP GAUGES, FUEL & OIL PRESSURE GAUGES, OIL TEMP GAUGES
14. PORT CONSOLE: EMERGENCY ELECTRICAL SUPPLY SELECTOR, IGNITION SWITCHES, PATIN COURSE CHANGE SELECTOR, CENTRAL WARNING PANEL, UNDERCARRIAGE, FLAP, DIVE BRAKE, BOMB DOORS, SELECTOR BOX, EMERGENCY ENGINE CUT-OUT HANDLES, EMERGENCY GEAR, FLAPS, DOORS CONTROLS, ENGINE STARTER SWITCHES
15. RUDDER, AILERON, ELEVATOR TRIM TAB CONTROL
16. TAIL WHEEL CASTOR LOCK

A HEAVILY ARMED ME 410B-2/U2/R4.

MESSERSCHMITT
Me 163

SMALL, AGILE, AND WITH TWICE THE SPEED OF PISTON-ENGINE FIGHTERS,
THE ME 163 WAS THE MOST SPECTACULAR INTERCEPTOR
TO SEE SERVICE DURING THE SECOND WORLD WAR.

The first Me 163 was completed as a glider and towed by a Messerschmitt Bf 110. The handling characteristics of the new glider were so good that it consistently refused to land. For security reasons, the first rocket-powered trials took place at Peenemunde. The engine used in the early flights developed a thrust of 1,653 pounds and the world speed record of 469.22 miles per hour (755 km/h) was easily eclipsed (wartime security prevented the new record from being claimed). The flying characteristics of the rocket-powered Me 163A were excellent; it was the take-off and landing that proved to be a serious problem. The Me 163 was equipped with a wheeled dolly that was jettisoned once airborne, and landing was accomplished with a sprung skid. This proved hazardous for the pilot in two ways. First, on bumpy airfields, premature take-offs and bouncing on landing could cause spinal damage to the pilot. Second, due to shaking of the rocket's volatile propellants, the occasional explosion would occur.

The Me 163's greatest handicap, however, was its range. The limited duration of the rocket motor gave the Me 163 enough power to reach 13,000 feet (3,962 m) and a short, level flight. Once the fuel was exhausted, the Me 163 had to glide back to earth.

In 1941, priority was shifted away from the Me 163. It was not until 1943 that the improved Me 163B model would take flight. By then, USAAF daylight bombing raids were a growing concern. Albert Speer, Germany's Minister of Armaments, ordered the Me 163 to be mass-produced. Named the Komet, the short-range Me 163 was given the task of point defence for such targets as the vital oil refineries near Leipzig. The first operational group to fly the Me 163 was Erprobungskommando 16. Tactics for

attacking American bomber formations were adopted and refined. As enemy bombers approached, the Me 163s would scramble. Climbing nearly vertically, at 440 miles per hour (708 km/h), they would reach 37,000 feet (11,300 m) in just 5 minutes and 45 seconds. Directed by ground radar, the Me 163s would be guided to a position 3,000 feet (914 m) above the bombers. From there they would attack. As sound as the tactics were, the practice was far from stable. To begin with, there were many fatal training accidents. The two highly volatile fuels (C-Stoff and T-Stoff) were completely incompatible. When mixed together they would decomposed immediately into a high-temperature gas and explode. Fuelling the Me 163 required two separate trucks that had to be kept a half mile apart at all times. In between fuelings, everything, including the ground crew, had to be washed down with water to be made ready for the second truck.

The combat effectiveness of the Me 163 was extremely limited. To reach the bombers, the Me 163s first had to avoid the escorting Mustangs, Lightnings, and Thunderbolts. To accomplish this and reach the B-17s and B-24s, the Komets had to approach the bombers at around 580 miles per hour (933 km/h). This left them with only two and a half seconds for actual shooting, and little hope of success. In its first major engagement, five Komets took on 1,096 USAAF bombers, resulting in one B-17 being damaged.

By March 1945, Allied air superiority was complete. Although 300 Me 163s were ready for frontline service, only a small number from 1/JG 400 were able to intercept incoming raids. They destroyed a total of nine bombers, but lost 14 Me 163s in the attempts.

ABOVE: EARLY PRODUCTION MODEL 163B. *RIGHT*: PROTECTED BY HIS SPECIAL FLYING SUIT, AN ME 163 PILOT CLIMBS INTO HIS COCKPIT.
INSET: THE ONLY KNOWN PICTORIAL EVIDENCE OF A SUCCESSFUL KOMET ATTACK.

THE PILOT'S
P E R S P E C T I V E
CAPTAIN
RUDOLF OPITZ

The first time I flew the Me 163, I believe, was in October 1941, at Peenemunde. I then flew the 163B model on June 4, 1943. The cockpit in the B model was very comfortable. The visibility through the clear Plexiglas hood was unobstructed and very nice. I never heard any complaints about the 163 cockpit. Through the early test program of the 163, there were a number of issues dealing with the cockpit that were never completely cleared.

One of the tests we conducted dealt with the release of the canopy while in flight. Once the canopy was released, it would not separate from the aircraft. Instead, it would float about an inch above the aircraft, stuck in the boundary layer of the fuselage. If the pilot pushed up on the canopy, it would not move, because of the airflow. On subsequent flights, we carried a broomstick handle so we could push the front of the canopy up and out of the boundary layer. Later, a spring-loaded bolt was added, but it was only found to work at low speeds. In the final production aircraft, an explosive charge was used to blow the canopy clear.

The instrumentation in the Me 163 was simple and convenient, and was designed for VFR flight only. The cockpit was quite compact, so the instruments were grouped closed together and very easy to see. Pilots who flew the 163 had to wear a special flying suit to protect them from the hydrogen peroxide fuel. On the left and right side of the pilot were two fuel tanks. Because they were self-sealing, with the armoured nose, I was never too concerned about their placement. The bigger concern for me was the main tank, in behind the pilot, which was unprotected!

I would rate the Me 163 cockpit as quite good. It was compact and convenient, with great visibility. I had few problems or concerns when I flew it.

MESSERSCHMITT Me 163B
NATIONAL AVIATION MUSEUM, OTTAWA

1. FUEL TANK FEED
2. TRIM HANDWHEEL
3. PORT "T-STOFF" FUEL TANK
4. STARTER SWITCH
5. THROTTLE LEVER
6. EMERGENCY UNDERCARRIAGE JETTISON COCK
7. UNDERCARRIAGE EMERGENCY JETTISON PRESSURE GAUGE
8. TOW TUG RELEASE HANDLE
9. CANOPY LATCH
10. CANOPY RELEASE
11. MAIN LINE SWITCH
12. FUG 25A CONTROL UNIT
13. AIRSPEED INDICATOR
14. TURN AND BANK INDICATOR
15. VARIOMETER
16. ALTIMETER
17. RPM COUNTER
18. TEMPERATURE GAUGE
19. THRUST INDICATOR
20. THRUST INDICATOR
21. FLAP MANUAL PUMP
22. FLAP SELECTOR LEVER
23. CONTROL COLUMN
24. PLASTIC RUDDER PEDALS
25. UNDERCARRIAGE, LANDING SKID INDICATOR
26. 90-MM ARMOURED GLASS

OBERFELDWEBEL SCHUBERT BESIDE HIS KOMET.

MESSERSCHMITT
Me 262

ALTHOUGH ITS IMPACT WAS LARGELY PSYCHOLOGICAL, WHEN THE ME 262
FIRST APPEARED, ITS DESIGN WAS REVOLUTIONARY. AS THE WORLD'S FIRST
TURBOJET FIGHTER, IT LEFT ITS MARK NOT ONLY IN WAR, BUT ALSO IN PEACE.

In 1941, Germany was flush with victory and conquest. The idea of a new and revolutionary fighter replacing the existing Bf 109 and Fw 190 had little priority or urgency. It was in this atmosphere that the Me 262 was born. In April 1941, the first Me 262 took to the air. Before the introduction of the turbojet engine, the first Me 262 was powered by a 750-horsepower liquid-cooled Jumo engine mounted in the nose weapon bay. This ungainly arrangement proved to be a great opportunity, as it was soon realized that the Me 262's aerodynamics could be studied without the added anxiety of testing a new unproven powerplant. The results were startling. The Me 262, bigger and heavier than the Bf 109, and powered by a relatively weak piston engine, managed to achieve a higher speed. This proved that the new design was aerodynamically superior to any other German fighter in service.

The first flight of an Me 262 using turbojet power alone occurred on July 18, 1942. The flight lasted 12 minutes and was considered a great success. Soon after, Messerschmitt received contracts to produce a number of prototypes for further testing. On May 22, 1943, Adolf Galland flew the Me 262 for the first time. He described his flight as follows: "It was as though angels were pushing." He told Goering that with the Me 262 the Luftwaffe would have a marked advantage over all Allied piston-engine aircraft. On November 26, 1943, Hitler watched as the sleek, futuristic Me 262 was put through its paces. Suitably impressed, Hitler asked if the 262 could carry bombs. Indeed it could, and from that point on Hitler demanded the Me 262 be produced as a jet bomber. Hitler's directive inevitably delayed production; even so, the first production model—the Me 262A-1 *Schwalbe* ("Swallow")—was used as a fighter.

As a fighter, the Me 262 was a revolutionary step forward. With a speed of 540 miles per hour (869 m) at 20,000 ft (6,096 m), it was faster than anything the Allies had. In November 1944, USAAF daylight bombing raids were increasing in tempo. Hitler reacted by rescinding his earlier order and demanded thousands of Me 262 fighters. The first unit to fly the world's first operational jetfighter, Erprobungskommando 262, was made up of mainly Messerschmitt test pilots. Ekdo 262 had the dual role of training new pilots and intercepting high-flying Mosquito and Lightning photo-reconnaissance aircraft. Later, the Me 262 was used primarily against USAAF bomber formations. In October 1944, the first fighter unit was formed from the original Ekdo 262. Commanded by Major Walter Nowotny, the unit was equipped with 30 new aircraft; by the end of the month only 3 were operational. This high attrition rate was caused, not by enemy action, but by crashes, engine failure, and pilot inexperience.

As the German situation grew desperate, they tried to increase the output of 262s. Through the use of extensively dispersed and heavily camouflaged makeshift factories, the Germans managed to produce 1,433 262s. In the end, only a hundred or so actually saw service. The last 262 unit was commanded by General Galland. Jagdverband 44 comprised an elite group of handpicked pilots, many holders of the Knight's Cross. Using the Munich Augsburd Autobahn, JV44 managed to stay operational for one month and claimed 50 American bombers destroyed.

General Galland argued that if the Me 262 had been available operationally in the spring of 1943, the American daylight bombing campaign would have been stopped. In hindsight, this claim may have been true. In the end, the contribution of the Messerschmitt Me 262 was minimal.

RIGHT: ME 262A-1A OF JAGDGESCHWADER 7 AT PERLEBERG, APRIL 1945. INSET: P-51 GUN CAMERA PHOTO OF AN ME 262.

THE PILOT'S
P E R S P E C T I V E
COLONEL
KEN CHILSTROM
USAF (RET.)

W e had two Me 262s at Wright Field, and there were some down at Freeman Field. I flew the Me 262 10 or 12 times, and each flight was less than and hour. Everyone was intrigued with the Me 262, knowing that it was one of the first aircraft with Jumo 004 axial-flow engines. Ironically, the true weakness of the Me 262 was its engines. We regarded the Jumo 004 as a 15-hour engine. The metallurgy at the time was not up to standard, and as a result the engine life was limited. Galland wanted to use the 262 as a high-altitude interceptor, but Hitler wanted it as a bomber. At low altitude its performance was severely limited.

When I first sat in the Me 262 cockpit, I found it to be rather small and tight fitting, but very comfortable. That in itself tells you something. I never felt quite at home in the 109 cockpit. I really liked the Fw 190. That was really a fighter pilot's airplane. The 262 instrument panel was of a conventional layout. The flight instruments were on the left, with the engine instruments on the right. Of course, we changed some of the instruments in the cockpit, replacing the German ones with American. The control stick was equipped with several controls that you didn't find on American aircraft. In a lot of ways it was the precursor to the modern jetfighter control column. The canopy release lever was very distinctive, and the all-round visibility from the cockpit was excellent. There was no ejection seat, and not being pressurized, that was somewhat of a limitation. Adjusting to the 262 was not a problem. We checked out a number of pilots. Guys like Chuck Yeager, who only flew one or two flights, had no problems adjusting to the aircraft. I found no real difference between the Bf 109, Fw 190, and Me 262 cockpits. I would have felt quite comfortable flying into combat in the Me 262.

MESSERSCHMITT Me 262A-1A
USAF MUSEUM, DAYTON, OHIO

1. CONTROL COLUMN
2. MASTER ARMING BUTTON
3. R4M/BOMB RELEASE BUTTON
4. GUN BUTTON
5. AIRSPEED INDICATOR
6. TURN AND BANK INDICATOR COMBINED WITH ARTIFICIAL HORIZON
7. RATE OF CLIMB INDICATOR
8. SENSITIVE/COARSE ALTIMETER
9. REPEATER COMPASS
10. AFN INDICATOR
11. RPM INDICATOR
12. ENGINE EXHAUST TEMP GAUGES
13. OIL PRESSURE INDICATOR
14. FUEL SUPPLY GAUGE
15. FIRE SAFETY CUT-OUT SWITCHES
16. RUDDER PEDAL
17. FUSE SWITCHBOX
18. LEVER FOR TAILPLANE ADJUSTMENT
19. SWITCH LEVER FOR FUEL COCK BATTERY
20. POWER LEVER
21. OXYGEN FLOW
22. CONTROL UNIT FOR IFF (FUG 25)
23. JUNCTION BOX
24. SWITCH BOX FOR RATOG
25. SIGNAL FLARE FIRING GEAR
26. MAIN SWITCH BOARD
27. WINDSHIELD HEATING
28. NOSEWHEEL BRAKE HANDLE

ME 262A-1AS OF
ERPROBUNGSKOMMANDO 262.

"During the approach you were mainly occupied with routine tasks: checking instruments, switching over magnetos to check the plugs, watching the oil temperature, checking the boost pressure and, every so often, feeling automatically for parachute straps and oxygen mask. You were flying in formation with others to the left and right above you. Nevertheless you were alone, very much alone in your thundering glass-topped box, a prey to the thoughts and temptations that war brings. You still had some personal choice; you could still decide whether or not you were going to carry out the orders for the attack, whether or not you would remain with the formation until there was no pulling back from the battle. Was the engine a bit rough? Was it misfiring? Were the revs droppping? Engine trouble would be a plausible excuse for falling behind and having to turn back. It was a temptation to which all pilots were exposed. "

— JOHANNES STEINHOFF,
THE STRAITS OF MESSINA:
DIARY OF A FIGHTER COMMANDER

BIBLIOGRAPHY
BOOKS

Angelucci, Enzo and Paolo Matricardi. *Combat Aircraft of World War II: 1944–1945*. New York: Military Press, 1988.

Bishop, Edward. *Mosquito Wooden Wonder*. New York: Ballantine Books, 1971

Bowan, Martin W. *USAF Handbook: 1939–1945*. Mechanicsberg, PA: Stackpole Books, 1977.

Bowyer, Chaz and Armand van Ishoven. *Hurricane at War, Messerschmitt at War*. USA: The Promotional Reprint Company, 1993.

Caidin, Martin. *Flying Forts: The B-17 in World War II*. New York: Ballantine, 1968.

———. *Fork-Tailed Devil: The P-38*. New York: Ballantine, 1971.

Cameron, Ian. *Wings of the Morning: The Story of the Fleet Air Arm in the Second World War*. London: Hodder & Stoughton, 1962.

Coombs, L. F. E. *The Aircraft Cockpit*. Northamptonshire, England: Patrick Stevens Limited, 1990.

David, Larry, et al. *P-35: Mini in Action*. Carrollton, Texas: Squadron/Signal Publications, 1994.

Donald, David, ed. *American Warplanes of World War II*. London: Aerospace Publishing, 1995.

———. *Warplanes of the Luftwaffe*. London: Aerospace Publishing, 1994.

Ethell, Jeffrey L. et al. *Great Book of World War II Airplanes*. Twelve volumes. New York: Bonanza Books, 1984.

Francillon, R. J. Ph D. *Japanese Aircraft of the Pacific War*. New York: Funk & Wagnalls.

Freeman, Roger A. *Mustang at War*. Garden City, New York: Doubleday, 1975.

Goodall, Geoff, and John Chapman. *Warbirds Worldwide Directory: An International Survey of the World's Warbird Population*. Mansfield, England: Warbirds Worldwide, 1989.

Green, William. *Famous Bombers of World War II*. Garden City, New York: Doubleday, 1959.

———. *Rocket Fighter*. London: Macdonald & Co., 1970.

———. *Warplanes of the Second World War: Fighters*. Volume 3. London: Macdonald & Co., 1961.

Gunston, Bill. *Classic Warplanes: North American P-51 Mustang*. Great Britain: Salamander Books, 1990.

———. *An Illustrated Guide to Bombers of World War II*. New York: Arco, 1980.

Halliday, Hugh A. *Typhoon and Tempest: The Canadian Story*. Toronto: CANAV Books, 1992.

Jablonski, Edward. *Airwar*. Garden City, New York: Doubleday, 1979.

Jane's Fighting Aircraft of World War II. New York: Avenel, 1994.

Johnson, Brian. *The Secret War*. London: British Broadcasting Corporation, 1978.

Kirk, John and Robert J. R. Young. *Great Weapons of World War II*. New York: Bonanza Books, **???**.

Mesko, Jim. *A-20: Havoc in Action*. Carrollton, Texas: Squadron/Signal Publications, 1994.

Polmar, Norman. *Aggressors: Carrier Power Vs. Fighting Ship*. Volume 2. New York: Zokesiha Publications, 1990.

Price, Alfred. *Classic Warplanes: Messerschmitt Bf 109*. Great Britain: Salamander Books, 1992.

———. *Spitfire at War*. London: Ian Allan, 1974.

Punka, George, and Joe Sewell. *Messerschmitt Me 210/410 in Action*. Carrollton, Texas: Squadron/Signal Publications, 1994.

Richardson, Doug. *Classic Warplanes: Boeing B-17 Flying Fortress*. Great Britain: Salamander Books, 1991.

Scutts, Jerry. *Typhoon Tempest In Action*. Carrollton, Texas: Squadron/Signals Publications, 1990.

Spick, Mike. *Classic Warplanes: Supermarine Spitfire*. Great Britain: Salamander Books, 1990.

Stanaway, John. *P-38: Lightning Aces of the Pacific and CBI*. Great Britain: Osprey Publishing, 1997.

Styling Mark. *Corsair Aces of World War II*. Great Britain: Osprey Publishing, 1995.

Tillman, Barrett. *Wildcat Aces of World War II*. Great Britain: Osprey Publishing, 1995.

———. *Hellcat Aces of World War II*. Great Britain: Osprey Publishing, 1995.

Weal, John. *Focke-Wulf Fw 190: Aces of the Western Front*. Great Britain: Osprey Publishing, 1996.

Vader, John. *Pacific Hawk*. New York: Ballantine Books Inc., 1970

Vanags-Baginskis, Alex. *Aggressors: Tank Buster Vs. Combat Vehicle*. Volume 1. New York: Zokesiha Publications, 1990.

PERIODICALS

"Beaufighter." *Air Enthusiast International*. March 1974.

Brown, Eric. "Swordfish: An Amiable Anachronism." *Air International*. March 1979.

Brown, Eric. "The Doughty Dauntless." *Air International*. October 1979.

"The Contentious Cobra." *Air International*. February 1982.

Ethell, Jeffery. "Flying the P-38 Lightning." *Flight*. August 1997.

"Fighting Juggernaut." *Air International*. January 1978.

"Fighting Juggernaut: Part Two." *Air International*. February 1978.

Francillon, Rene J. "Profile 213: Kawanishi K1K Kyofu/Rex & Shiden/George." Profile Publications Limited.

"Hawk Monoplanes: The Second Generation." *Air International*. March 1977.

"The Last Swallow of Summer: The Extraordinary Story of the Ki-100." *Air International*. October 1977.

Shores, Christopher. "The RAF's Loss-Leader." *Diamond Jubilee Royal Air Force Yearbook*. 1978.

"Airacomet...A Jet Pioneer by Bell." Air International. March 1980

"Sea Hurricane-Shipboard Fighter Extempore." Air International. September 1978

INDEX

PHOTOGRAPH CREDITS

LEGEND: I = INSET   M = MAIN

IMPERIAL WAR MUSEUM: 3, 16, 17(I,M), 18, 20, 21(I,M), 22, 24(I,M), 25 (I), 26, 28, 29, 30, 32, 33 (I,M), 36, 37(I), 38, 40, 41(M), 44, 46, 48, 50,   99, 119, 120, 126, 129, 164, 165(I,M), 166. JEFFERY L. ETHELL COLLECTION: 13, 41(I), 54, 58, 67(M), 72, 83, 87(I), 94, 107, 114, 118, 130. DAVE MENARD: 55. USAAF MUSEUM: 56, 66, 68, 78, 79, 103(I). LOCKHEED AIRCRAFT CORPORATION: 59 (I,M), 86, 87(M). NATIONAL AIR & SPACE MUSEUM: 9, 60, 62 (I,M), 64, 67(I), 71(I,M), 74, 75, 76, 82, 84, 91, 95, 98, 104, 103, 115, 153(I), 157(I), 158, 160(I,M), 169(I,M), 170. KEN CHILSTROM: 80. NATIONAL ARCHIVES: 90, 106 (I,M), 108, 110. 111(I,M), 112, 116, 132, 137(M). PHILLIP JARRETT: 124, 134, 137(I), 138, 142, 143, 144, 152, 162. BUNDESARCHIV: 148, 149, 153(M), 154, 156, 157(M), 173. JOHN WEAL: 150. GARY SANFORD: 10.